SH*T HAPPENS

SH*T HAPPENS

HAPPENS

Lessons for dealing with
life's ups and downs

Kyle MacDonald

upstart press

A catalogue record for this book is available from the National Library of
New Zealand

ISBN 978-1-99000367-7
eISBN 978-1-990003-99-8

An Upstart Press Book
Published in 2023 by Upstart Press Ltd.
26 Greenpark Road, Penrose, Auckland 1061
New Zealand

Design and illustration by Nick Turzynski, redinc. Book design, www.redinc.co.nz.

Printed on demand by IPG.

Contents

Introduction

FOR OVER TWENTY YEARS I have sat in a chair and listened as people talked about their childhoods, their addictions, their sex lives (or lack of them), their pain, their traumas, their loves and losses, their dreams and their aspirations. After so many years I sometimes forget that these are conversations they may have never had before, and to talk openly like we do in my room is not something people do in day-to-day life.

I'm not a religious person, but over time a therapy relationship becomes a sacred space.

If you've come here looking for juicy work stories, I won't be sharing anyone else's secrets. Trust and confidentiality are the cornerstones of what enables therapy to work — so you won't be reading any "client's details changed to protect their confidentiality" type titbits from me.

Instead, this is my story, of what I've learned about life, emotions and how we function — or don't — from my clients.

As therapists, we are of course trained to listen. We are also trained to do things that are helpful with the aim of alleviating intense psychological pain, the aftereffects of trauma, the emptiness of depression, and the unbearable tension of anxiety. Most people come to therapy because there is a clear problem to be solved, what therapists refer to as "the symptom(s)".

But curing "the symptom" rarely ends up being the only, or even the most important, outcome of therapy.

Given the opportunity to talk, and unravel themselves and their struggles, most people find they want a deeper understanding of themselves, and in doing so to find deeper meaning in their lives.

To sit in a chair for two decades listening to people talk about their lives you have to find the human condition fascinating. It helps to be what I often describe as, "psychotically optimistic". Life's tough. Even if you feel things have gone well for you, there's still grief, breakups, and accidents — not to mention global pandemics — to navigate.

The limited nature of life, and the fact we all stare down death — at one time or another — means no one finds this being alive business a walk in the park.

So, while various therapists, with their different approaches, will try to tell you the secret, or teach you various techniques to "help" — most of which are both useful *and* oversold — fundamentally we all must find our own ways to ease the pain of being, and make the journey of being alive a little more bearable.

And when push comes to shove, the only thing that helps is other people. This can be tricky if it's also true that if your experience of other people is that they are also the problem. They often are.

Basically, this is how therapy helps. Not the techniques, the worksheets, the apps, the clever tricks, the new theories, or the psychobabble. It's much simpler than that. Just having a consistent, attentive and validating person to whom you can express yourself freely and figure out what life means, takes us a long way towards where we need to be.

That doesn't mean that anyone can do it. There is an old saying in design that making something look simple is incredibly complicated. The same goes for therapy. Even if it might look simple, it's actually hard work to be fully present to someone else, day in and day out. That's why it's a job —

albeit an enjoyable and deeply satisfying one.

So, this isn't really a "self-help" book (even though that is likely where it will land in bookshops). From the point of view of therapy "self-help" is an anathema. We only get so far on our own before we need someone else.

In life "Shit" unavoidably happens. Of this, I can be absolutely certain. It is then up to us what we make of it. All of us have habits, built up over many years, of what we do with the "shit".

Based on how honed our capacity to regulate — to feel but not get overwhelmed by our emotions — we will respond to situations in ways that are regulated or dysregulated. If we respond in a dysregulated way when we are overwhelmed, our emotions tend to take over the steering wheel. And emotions on their own generally aren't great drivers.

Depending on a wide range of factors, we will also be able to react in a flexible, accepting, and even creative manner to the shit. Or we may be the kind of person who relies on controlling what we can — or, problematically, trying to control even more. These four factors (regulation/ dysregulation, flexible/inflexible) interact, much like the points on a compass. Understanding these four responses to what life throws at us and how they interact, can help us better navigate our world.

So, think of this more as a map than a self-help book. Or a smorgasbord of helpful things I've learnt along the way. Because there is no shortage of techniques out there you can employ that may be helpful.

Hopefully, this map that I unfurl in front of you will show you some things that people learn in therapy, and then help you be more selective in the ways you approach your emotional world.

A map that is easier to use when we understand our own tendency to be regulated or dysregulated, flexible or rigid. That helps us understand our need for control or our unhealthy attraction to chaos, and how much easier it all becomes when those things are in balance.

A map that might lead you to more satisfying relationships in your life, with others, yourself — or maybe even with a therapist.

CHAPTER 1:
Are we all a bit mad?

IN CHARLES DICKENS'S *A Christmas Carol* the main character, Ebenezer Scrooge is visited by ghosts who attempt to show him the error of his ways. Ultimately the only thing that helps him to see the impact of his heartless, wealth-focused life is the very real prospect of his death, and the view afforded him of what his life might look like from his deathbed.

Most of us spend very little time contemplating our mortality — and with good reason. Denial of death and the ability to set aside our mortality helps us to live unencumbered with dark thoughts about the finite nature of our existence. One of the features of clinical depression is a focus on death: either excessive thoughts about it or contemplating it in the form of suicide.

However, considering death — as Scrooge is forced to by the ghost of Christmas Future — can sometimes be helpful.

Perhaps the pre-eminent writer in terms of psychotherapy and death is Dr Irvin Yalom. He's written books that most therapists have probably read — largely because they're very well written (yes, I am a bit of a fan).

In his seminal text *Existential Psychotherapy* and his more recent — and more accessible — *Staring at the Sun* he writes at length about the way people's experiences of terminal illness shape not just how they see themselves and their lives, but what they consider to be important. And in what can almost seem like a cliché now, he encourages us all to contemplate the question:

"If you knew you only had six months to live, how would you choose to spend your time?"

What would you do or not do? Who would you spend it with — and what would you want to say to them?

And who would you want to hold you when you finally slip away?

I hope you will come away from this book understanding there are no easy answers or silver bullets. But when it comes to considering what really matters, knowing how we want to feel when we die is one of the surest ways of informing how we want to live.

The problem of psychiatry

Over the twenty years I have been doing this therapy thing, there has been a significant and necessary shift in the way we talk about mental health — almost all of it for the better.

Destigmatisation campaigns have made it more possible for people to be open about their struggles. And the general level of knowledge about emotional health, depression, addictions and anxiety is a world away from what it was at the end of last century.

Yet at the same time, in the countries that measure such things, rates of depression, anxiety and other mental health disorders have increased, year on year, along with rates of suicide.

The recent pandemic and its multitude of impacts are likely to see this trend continue, even accelerate.

So, are we getting "worse"? Or is something else going on? Well, annoyingly it's likely both. There is little question that events like the ongoing Covid-19 pandemic have had widespread impacts. But it is also true that as we have all become more familiar with previously medically defined psychiatric conditions, like depression, panic attacks, and OCD, these terms have entered our day-to-day understanding in ways that may be helpful, and unhelpful.

It's well recognised that when people start studying what used to be called "Abnormal Psychology" or psychiatric diagnosis (most commonly in Aotearoa that means the "DSM" or *Diagnostic and Statistical Manual of Mental Disorders*) we see ourselves, and our quirks in the categories of diagnosis in its pages. Undergraduate psychology students routinely decide they have any number of psychiatric disorders they weren't aware of!

They're usually wrong. Why? Because in simple terms, for any of those things to be considered a problem, they have to, well, actually cause problems. Models of psychiatric classification (and yes there is more than one and they do differ) are not diagnosing medical, quantifiable physiological disease. They are inherently subjective, and prone to error, debate, disagreement and cultural bias. While in the main they offer a useful and reliable map, they are an invention of humans and should be viewed with a smidge of cynicism.

This is not to say, however, that the conditions and distress they attempt to imperfectly describe are not "real". They most certainly are. But simply put, they describe human experiences of distress and pain, and in doing so we can all find aspects of ourselves contained within their pages.

For example, you might prefer tidiness and order. I know I do. I prefer my office, and generally, my home to be tidy. I prefer neat stacks, and things laid out well, and am not a fan of clutter. If there is a mess, it winds me up — and if I feel particularly stressed out, I can even clean up as a way to manage my stress. I find it easier to be calm in an ordered space, and I can get a bit rigid when under stress.

This does not mean I have "OCD" (obsessive-compulsive disorder) — even though that is a diagnosis that is increasingly misused to describe people who prefer tidiness and order. (Technically — and somewhat confusingly — this would actually be "Obsessive Compulsive Personality Disorder" and I don't have that either.) OCD is *not* about tidiness. It's about behaviours — compulsions — that people need to do, often repeatedly, to reduce an intense fear of a dreaded outcome. The death of a loved one for instance.

Simply put, managing my emotions and the spaces I live in in this way doesn't cause me a problem. While I can tend to be a bit rigid when stressed, I can also be flexible, and tolerate mess and clutter when I need to — or have to. In terms of diagnosis, I can still live, love and work — and for something to technically be considered a "mental illness" it has to cross one of those thresholds. Namely it needs to cause problems in terms of our ability to work, to have and maintain intimate relationships and/or friendships, and impair our day-to-day functioning in the world.

We all have our ways of regulating our emotions, and you likely are familiar with yours. For example, you may be someone who needs people around them or conversely needs to be alone to process feelings. You may exercise to manage distressing feelings or need to retreat under the duvet with nothing but Netflix for company. You may prefer to eat when stressed, or find your appetite diminishes when faced with unexpected challenges. You may tend towards more rigid approaches, or find you need to freely express yourself and be a bit more flexible in your regulating strategies. Most of us have a mix of both.

These coping strategies, or what psychotherapists sometimes call "defences" — internal and external strategies to manage distress and painful emotional states — are not necessarily pathological. We all have them, and they are normal and necessary ways of managing our emotional lives.

Again, they're only a problem if they're a problem.

Throughout this book it's safe to assume that if I'm using a clinical term — say addiction or depression for instance — I'm meaning it in a clinical sense.

I think it's important to find new ways to talk about distress and differences without pathologising everyday human experiences. There are some exceptions, but my view is that we need to resist what some people see as "concept creep". For instance, broadening the terms we use to describe psychiatric disorders to include more and more everyday versions of human behaviour — as in my liking of order. Another example of this is when we utilise terms like "trauma" to describe almost any upsetting event, thereby pathologising distressing emotions and experiences.

Language matters when it comes to how we organise our experience, how we describe what is happening inside ourselves to others, and how we define ourselves and our identity.

When a problem is a problem

When feelings overwhelm our capacity to think, and perceive ourselves or the world around us, then it's a problem.

Everyone comes to therapy to solve problems, and most of those problems can be traced back to how we regulate (or don't) our emotions. I'll cover this in much more detail later, but in simple terms, we all have the capacity to tolerate a certain level of emotions. And all emotions can come to dominate our thoughts and shift how we perceive reality — if they're strong enough.

In general, our internal experience can get so distorted by our distress and how we perceive it, we can experience things that aren't experienced by others, e.g., hallucinations and voices. If this is chronic and disturbing enough, we call this psychosis — a break from consensual reality.

If our feelings distort how we experience other people's intents, motives or behaviour, or mean we experience our emotional states as unquestionably real, and struggle to have insight into those distortions (for instance, intense jealousy in response to a faithful partner) then generally we call it emotional dysregulation. In its most severe forms, where all aspects of our lives are impacted, we think of this as a personality disorder. The most well-known personality disorders are "borderline personality disorder" and "narcissistic personality disorder". Being most well-known also means they are the most likely to be thrown around willy-nilly in a clear example of concept creep.

Generally, if we feel things intensely enough that it influences our behaviour — for instance, we avoid situations that cause us distress — then we call it a "neurotic" disorder. An example of this is social anxiety. The feelings are intense, but with neurotic disorders people have insight into the fact that it's their feelings that are the problem.

Incidentally, Freud described the aim of therapy as not being cured but achieving "normal neurosis".

What I've just described above — psychotic disorders, personality disorders, and neurotic disorders — is a way of thinking of the severity of psychological distress from modern psychodynamic theory, the family of theories that I'm largely trained in as a psychotherapist. It's a map, and like any map, it's a representation of reality, which is more or less accurate.

Psychodynamic theories are a broad family of theories. Originating with Freud, they have evolved to understand in broad terms that the emotional environment that we grow up in — and the first relationships we have with our parents and caregivers — shape our emotional development, for good, bad and everything in between. I'll take this up more soon, but it's important to say here that while Freud gets much criticism from many of the social sciences — and not entirely without reason — when we talk about psychodynamic psychology it has developed a lot since the early twentieth century. And to be fair to the good doctor, many ideas we now take for granted — the importance of early attachment relationships and the value of the first three years of life for instance — are cornerstones of psychodynamic thinking.

It's also true that much of what we will talk about when it comes to the impact of early life is about influence, as opposed to trauma and pathology. We all have a family, we are all shaped by our environment, and from that place, we all develop ways of coping with the world. Being shaped is not the same as being traumatised. Being influenced and developing ways of coping with the world is not necessarily pathological — it's only a problem if it's a problem.

And yes, this way of categorising human experiences and difficulties is as flawed as the rest of them, and not without its problems and criticisms.

For instance, we now understand much more about the influence of genetics on our responses to the environment we find ourselves in, and epigenetics — where our environment can shape our genes. And we also understand that cultural differences play a large part in the ways emotional distress is expressed.

You're probably familiar with various campaigns over the years that quote statistics like, "one in five people experience mental illness", and while the exact proportions may vary, the message remains the same. At any time probably more people than you would think are struggling with intense distress. It "unhides" the problem.

They were helpful campaigns, no doubt. However, it's also

true that those ways of presenting the data can still lead to "othering" — I'm normal, but those people over there are struggling. Distress, mental illness, and depression are still things only a small number of people suffer from.

What, in my view, is more illuminating, is the data from the world-leading study taking place here in our backyard — the Dunedin Longitudinal Study. Having tracked around 1000 people for just over 50 years — and still going — they were able to show that around 80 percent of people will at some point in their life experience mental illness if you include addictions to alcohol and other drugs.

To put that another way, four out of five people will at some point in their life struggle in ways that are serious enough to interfere with their day-to-day lives.

Maybe so-called "abnormal" psychology — what studying psychological diagnosis and psychiatry was called when I did my degree — isn't so abnormal after all?

Wellbeing and the dangerous myth of "normal"

One of the biggest problems with trying to define "abnormal" is it implies the existence of a "normal". A healthy, stable, calm being that we might aspire to be.

The perfectly balanced, emotionally healthy human.

It's not uncommon for people who land in therapy to believe that everyone else has it together. Happy marriages, healthy children, and successful careers. Regular trips to the gym, and a balanced diet. Contentment. Success. Two-point-four children, and a picket fence.

I understand how it can seem that way. Social media — and Instagram in particular — does us no favours here, with its tendency to present the holiday snaps of our day-to-day lives in a montage of smiling mediocrity, the complicated reality of life taking place off camera. Of course, even before social media, we've always tended to keep the reality of our lives hidden, to mask up, say things are "fine" when people ask how we are. To all walk around like there's nothing wrong. It's a necessary skill, even if it does mean to some extent, we're all hiding.

But I truly believe the idea of normal is not only a myth but a deeply dangerous myth. A myth promulgated by advertising agencies trying to sell us sugar-laden carbonated water that will bring us spiritual fulfilment.

And of course, in good late 20th-century fashion, people figured out how to utilise that insecurity, that worry there might be something "wrong" with us — for profit. As a business model, it has always existed in one form or another. And I'd be re-writing history to suggest that there isn't an overlap between the history of psychotherapy, and the self-help and wellbeing industry.

But whether it's the 1970s and self-actualisation, the second-hand bookshops awash in self-help books, or the more recent online world of wellbeing influencers with a silver bullet secret that will set you on the path to Nirvana, they're all cut from the same cloth.

There is no shortcut, and in many ways, there is no secret. All these approaches are fundamentally flawed because they seek to defend against the truth of the messiness, pain and at times outright despair of living a complicated, mortal, messy, human life.

There isn't really any such thing as "self-help" in the way it's marketed to us because you can't do it on your own. That's why I never wanted to write a self-help book. And why this isn't one.

If you start by trying to help yourself, you're looking in the wrong place. We find ourselves in each other, in connection with other humans. Good psychotherapy understands this and indeed utilises the relationship between client and therapist to facilitate self-understanding — to see who you are, how you behave and why — more clearly.

The flaw with all self-improvement is it starts from a place of assuming there's something wrong with you. That the fix is to be "better" — more independent, make more money, be more forceful, more patient, more kind, or whatever the current cultural trend about these things might be.

That's not to say that ideas, books and thoughts aren't helpful. But they do have their limits. And any self-help you read should hopefully lead you back to a deeper connection with those around you. And seeing more, hearing more and understanding more about the reality of lives for others is an amazingly helpful spin-off of being more open and connected.

Since 2014, I've had the privilege of being the co-host of a radio show called "The Nutters Club" here in Aotearoa. It has a simple mission: to change attitudes towards mental distress by telling stories. Every day people share their experiences of mental illness, addiction, grief, trauma and suicide. How they got there, and what they did to move on with their lives. Stories of hope, because hope — as we say on the show — is the key to life.

The more we know about other's stories the more we're able to contextualise and normalise our own experiences.

One of the differences between the show and doing therapy is I get to hear more of what happens next. Most people move on from therapy as soon as they can, as they should. But it does mean as a therapist, it's a bit like reading two-thirds of a book and not finding out how the story ends.

And one of the main things that stands out from hearing people's experiences, is that it's less about the "diagnosis" or the label. For some, that's a start, and it can be a very helpful start — but ultimately what helps people, and gives them a reason to keep working at the hard bits of managing

not considering the differences between people well enough, and treating the healthy male body as its definition of normal. Psychiatry is also having its own reckoning, and long may it last.

This sort of thinking is what some might consider "intersectionality" the idea that each of these differences come together — or intersect — in individuals and lead to an experience of oppression and marginalisation that creates their unique experience, for good and or ill. Like most things to do with race and difference, it provokes strong reactions in people. Nonetheless, it does start to make sense of the fact that if you are marginalised, due to your sexuality, your gender identity, your ethnicity or your gender, you are more likely to experience mental ill health than the population average.

Perhaps it's society that's mad?

All of this should inform not only any therapy but also any attempts to work towards accepting ourselves. You may or may not have felt accepted and valued growing up. You may have felt different, less than or strange. You may still feel that way about yourself.

But know that those judgements have come from somewhere — outside of you. They don't have to be you. And while it's too easy to have thoughts and opinions on what others should think about themselves, and what is the right way to be, think, behave, or emote, we learn more when we take the time to listen. Because there is no such thing as normal, no such thing as neurotypical, and no perfect way to get from birth to death without accumulating some pain along the way.

But I genuinely believe when we work at self-acceptance and self-compassion, we also are more open to the different experiences of people around us, and hopefully, less likely to inflict those judgements on others as well. Because yes, we are all mad, and yes, society is too.

But unavoidably, society is us.

SUMMARY

- Beware the tendency as you learn more about yourself to self-diagnose in order to describe yourself.
- "It's only a problem if it's a problem": your unique way of being you is only a "diagnosis" if it causes problems in your day-to-day life.
- We all have ways of managing — or regulating — our emotions. Too much rigidity or too much flexibility in our responses can be a problem. The aim is balance and doing only what is needed.
- There is no such thing as normal. It's an abstract idea not well suited to describing our unique makeup as emotional human beings.
- There is no such thing as "self-help". We all need others to help us figure ourselves, and life, out.

CHAPTER 2:
Surviving childhood and parenting

AT SOME POINT in the first couple of sessions — if it hasn't already come up — I ask every person I meet with, "So, tell me about your childhood ...?"

It can be a difficult question, and for good reason; talking about our experiences of childhood can feel tricky, vulnerable, shameful or maybe just irrelevant.

But you can also tell quite a bit by how people answer such a seemingly simple question: "It was fine ... I had a completely normal childhood ... ", "I had a perfectly happy childhood ...", "Now, let me tell you about my MOTHER!", or "I don't really remember much about my childhood."

No one had a normal childhood — but it can be easy to feel that whatever our experience our childhood was "normal". It was normal to us, and we only know what we know.

Of course, this doesn't mean the opposite is true — that everyone had a difficult or traumatic childhood. And when I ask people about their childhood, I always reassure them this isn't an exercise in looking for problems or blaming their parents. But it is a search for understanding and being able to lay out the influences that impacted how you developed emotionally. For good, for bad, and perhaps — unfortunately — for ill.

The environment we grow up in shapes us, in much the same way a tree root will grow around a rock in the ground. When you shape Bonsai, you take advantage of this, knowing that if you remove the rock, the shape of the tree then remains the same.

So, what are the big influences on our development, how do they shape us and in what ways might — at least some of it — be your parent's fault?

Attachment and beginnings

Human newborns are completely useless. It's because of our big brains: we have to be born before we can do very much at all. If, like giraffes, we were born with our brains more developed and ready to run around moments after we were born, we wouldn't be born at all because our heads wouldn't fit out through the birth canal. If you've given birth, then you know it's pretty touch and go already!

It's also true that baby humans are kind of annoying, and hard work — because they're so useless. In constant need of protection, feeding, cleaning. Digestive systems that barely work, and a cry that can set your teeth on edge.

Yet for almost all of us who become parents, we experience the most overwhelming and profound sense of love and desire to protect our children from the moment we first hold them.

That's the oxytocin high. We think love evolved to make up for our lack of any skills whatsoever — apart from being adorable, perhaps. A love that needed to be so blind and so overwhelmingly powerful we happily put up with the most ridiculous nonsense for years on end before we have an even vaguely useful human on our hands.

Oxytocin, often referred to as the love hormone — although like any brain hormone it's not quite that simple

— is triggered by childbirth, breastfeeding, social bonding, positive physical contact and in adult love, sex.

Attachment is a term that loosely describes that early bond between baby and parents (originally coined by John Bowlby in the 1950s, it tends to just refer to "mother") and its glue is oxytocin. Its function is of course survival, but it's also true that some very important bedrock of our emotional development is laid in those first few months and years. Emotional regulation, in particular, is how we learn — or don't — to soothe ourselves and regulate our emotional world. Many animals display bonding behaviours — think of the many examples of birds or other animals who bond to a human who "hatches" them.

But human attachment is, like us, more complicated.

Parenting a baby is fundamentally an emotional process. When we as parents respond to our children attentively, in a way that regulates them, makes sense of their cries and provides them with what they need, then we lay another building block on their capacity to regulate their own emotional states. And despite the inevitable worry and guilt we might feel at times, we don't have to get it right all the time. As famous child psychotherapist, Donald Winnicott said — it just needs to be (on average) "good enough".

One of the temptations with therapy and talking about our childhoods is to go looking for one-off traumatic incidents that explain everything. There is no question that trauma can have a big impact on development, but even with trauma what is important is the emotional background within which it occurs.

So, this would tend to suggest that it is your mother's — or father's — fault, wouldn't it? If their approach isn't "good enough"? If they don't respond, on average, in an emotionally responsive manner? Maybe, but where did they learn — or not learn — to manage their own emotions, and therefore respond effectively? I'll talk more about compassion, forgiveness and blame later, but for now, you can see the problem: Where does it end? Who's fault is it? When I became a parent I had a simple goal (and I hold all parents to this expectation): to do a better job than my parents did. Improve on their efforts.

Be good enough.

The power of validation

"Calm down!!" never works. Most of us know this and know what it feels like to be on the receiving end of being told to calm down, stop crying, chill out, etc.

And yet we all do it and will likely do it again at some point. This is "invalidation", or more specifically invalidation by oversimplifying the problem: the solution to being upset is just to calm down!

Any action that tells us that what we're feeling, thinking, or experiencing is wrong, too much or too intense is invalidating. And the main problem is it just doesn't work. Being told to calm down in the middle of an argument is likely to have the completely opposite impact.

So, when we talk about "good enough" emotional parenting we're also talking about being, on average, validating. In other words, being able to respond to the emotional states of our children with the message that what they feel is understandable, acceptable and valid.

We do this through words: "Of course you're upset!", "Oh, that looks really sore . . .", or "I get you're angry . . . I'd feel that way too in your situation."

We also do it through actions. By giving a hug, and a comforting arm, responding to their cries for attention or food, and reassuring them with our presence.

Over time, if this validation is "good enough" then we

take that in, and we learn to respond to ourselves in a validating way.

This is what therapists call "internalising". Hopefully, once we are out at the other end of childhood we end up with an internal voice that is largely validating and helps us to regulate our emotional responses. In reality, for most of us it's more like we have the cartoon devil on one shoulder and an angel on the other. At different times we might be able to be validating or invalidating toward ourselves. But again, the key is on average is it good enough?

The good news is that being more validating is a learnable skill. The bad news is that it also relies on our own ability to tolerate the emotions we have in response to others. Most of the time when any of us aren't being our best selves and are invalidating our partner, our children, or our friends it's because we're not tolerating what's happening inside us — emotionally speaking. We might blame them by invalidating them, "you're just being too emotional about it!" but it's ourselves, and our responses we're struggling with.

This is all to say that any effort to learn to be more validating of others must go hand in hand with efforts to get more comfortable with our own feelings.

So over time, the "average" approach of our caregivers sets the foundations for how we respond to ourselves — more, or less, validating.

We have to acknowledge here the general impact of temperament, or if you prefer, genetics. And no, this is not going to be an exercise in re-hashing the old "nature versus nurture" debate, because it's never that simple. The more we learn about the impact of the environment, we also understand that genetics aren't fixed.

It would be more accurate to say that our nature is expressed *via* nurture — in an ongoing feedback loop. And it's also hard to know where exactly to draw the line. If for instance, we're quite an emotional person (we tend to feel things more and are more aware of, and sensitive to, our feeling states) then this does seem to be about temperament. Babies seem to be born more, or less, emotional from the get-go. If as parents we aren't always great at validating ourselves, then if we have an emotional baby, it's going to be hard to be as attentive as we might need to be, therefore passing on the same — learned — pattern.

It's always hard to say where the line is between nature and nurture, but it is clear that these patterns get passed down from one generation to another. And remember, we're not necessarily talking about trauma or anything we might frame as harmful — just the emotional climate of our early years that shapes the person we become.

One of the ways of measuring if the emotional climate was a problem, is to return to attachment.

How secure are you?

Attachment theory first outlined three main attachment styles and later added a fourth.

"Secure Attachment", which research has fairly consistently shown over the years accounts for around two-thirds of the population. Secure attachment is marked by a good enough experience, where we can have and maintain relationships and manage the inevitable ups and downs. I like to think of secure attachment as being defined by being able to "use" our relationships to regulate ourselves emotionally. So, when we're upset, we turn to our parents, and later our partners and other relationships, and they are generally helpful. People who are securely attached will give a reasonably balanced view of their childhood when asked and can expand on details when questioned.

The remaining third of the population is what we call

"Insecurely Attached". Attachment theory describes two sub-types of insecure attachment. First, is "Avoidant Attachment", where the early relationships are marked by parenting styles that tends to judge or criticise "neediness" and push too fast and too soon for independence because that's what is valued. The relationship may be distant, cold, or not very emotionally engaged. This tends to lead to adults who are dismissive of the importance of intimacy and emotions, and will be more likely to say when asked "how was your childhood?" — "Fine, my parents are great people, I had a wonderful childhood." However, when pushed they tend to struggle with, or won't, expand on the details.

The second insecure attachment style is "Ambivalently Attached" which is characterised by parenting that may be present and attentive, but out of sync with babies' emotional needs. These parents tend to escalate their child's distress and over-respond to fear and anxiety. This leads to children that may seem "clingy" compared to their peers, and struggle to develop age-appropriate independence.

As adults, the ambivalently attached tend to be angry and stuck in feelings about their parents. They will definitely feel it's their mother's fault and will struggle to manage themselves in relationships and blame others for their upset and struggles. They tend to have no trouble outlining the things their parents got wrong, and will likely, quite understandably, be upset about it. However, they will likely also have trouble setting boundaries, and managing or moving away from their parents, even if the relationship is still harmful, upsetting and abusive. They are likely still tangled up with their family in ways that cause ongoing problems.

Lastly, and added a little while after the initial research outlined the three previous categories, is "Disorganised Attachment". This group is, as the name suggests, unable to maintain or have any consistent patterns in their close relationships and sadly have usually experienced profound, serious and chronic abuse from a very young age. Their lives as adults are severely disrupted by alcohol, drugs and mental illness and they may struggle to manage their lives at all.

Attachment patterns are not a life sentence, however. They can change. And as we age, these patterns get more complex, and you may see parts of yourself in more than one attachment style. Attachment styles are a useful "map" for understanding and potentially changing our behaviour. More generally all our collective experiences in life help us form an idea of ourselves. The way others relate to us, and the way we're talked to (and talked about), teaches us what to think about ourselves.

You are what you hear

There's a famous scene in the movie *Good Will Hunting* where the therapist character played by the late, great, Robin Williams repeatedly tells his young client Will — played by Matt Damon — "It's not your fault" until he breaks down in tears and change miraculously happens.

Feeling like you're always to blame for what goes wrong in your relationships is common with the experience of many with depression, and it incapacitates people. In the face of bad treatment from others, in the grip of distress, rejection, or hurt, it causes us to collapse. Unable to fight, we instead fall into despair.

See, everyone knows you're bad. Everyone knows it's your fault.

Good Will Hunting may have acted out on screen an unrealistic solution to Will's despair and shame, but it was right about the causes.

This is what we mean when people talk about the "self-critic" or negative self-talk.

Children's worlds are small, and they naturally place

and enforced when we can remain relatively calm and clear.

Because while many approaches will focus on the discipline and the boundaries part of the equation, actually it is always the relationship we need to prioritise.

Part of being able to balance all this is being clear about what is and isn't possible, with the most well-known example being that of youthful impulsiveness. It is true that the part of the brain that helps us as a species to regulate our behaviour — the handbrake if you like — is the last part of the brain to fully develop. Called the pre-frontal cortex, it is the part of the brain situated just above the eyebrows. However, like most things, it's not as simple as the teen brain *making* them impulsive. People have their own individual levels of impulsiveness and adventurousness.

Impulsiveness is generally fuelled by emotion. By definition, to be impulsive is to follow our emotional urges, our desires, despite our rational thoughts. Strong emotions make us more impulsive. As we've already discussed, many aspects of our emotional development — including our temperament — can lead to us having trouble regulating strong emotions, and so drive impulsivity.

Which of course brings us back to validation and connection.

Trying to have too much authority over our teens doesn't tend to work even though once we get ourselves to that "rigid–inflexible" place (see page 246),it can feel "right". Just telling anyone to, "calm down", "stop being impulsive", "don't be silly", or asking, "what did you do that for?" doesn't work very well for anyone, let alone teenagers. These responses are likely to cause more upset and dysregulated emotion and in doing so exacerbate the very problem we're hoping to solve.

The opposite of an authoritarian approach to teenagers who constantly push the boundaries and appear "oh so grown up", is what has been dubbed "Laissez-Faire" parenting. This pretty much equates to checking out and being too (in a developmental sense) permissive. Laissez-fair parenting has its now very obvious dangers. Like many mistakes it is possible to innocently make as a parent, this approach is a failure to match one's parenting interventions with the developmental stage of the child. It can be seductive to back off in the face of the conflict and relational demands of parenting, perhaps your parents did the same thing. But it is a very pernicious, even if mostly unintentional, form of neglect. To expect — or worse demand — a young person to just do what they can't yet do — manage themselves in the world and be responsible — is setting everyone up for failure.

As the neuropsychologists would put it — you're trying to have a conversation with a part of the brain that doesn't exist yet.

The middle path between authoritarian — too much discipline — and laissez-faire styles, is to coach, guide and explain limits in a straightforward and fact-based way. Be consistent and clear, but also be prepared to be flexible and creative. But most importantly, be good enough, and don't be afraid to make mistakes or take measured risks. Being good enough at parenting teens is about being willing to be human, and to be vulnerable and talk about our own mistakes, and perhaps most importantly, being able to say sorry.

As with most things, this is all very easy to say, but if it is particularly hard to implement then it is worth reflecting on what the challenges are for you. We are all naturally prone to repeat — for good or ill — or to be influenced by the parenting approach we received growing up. That might be literally doing the same thing, or alternatively rejecting the parenting we received and doing the opposite. The latter is what therapists call counter-identifying which can seem like trying to do something different but is still being bound by it, albeit in a different way.

If you notice you tend to get more rigid and controlling, then work on acceptance, staying in the moment and being creative and collaborative in your approaches. And if you tend to get distressed and emotional in response to your child's moods, then focus on slowing down, breathing, taking time to restore regulation and don't make decisions in the moment. Instead regulate before deciding, for example, "Give me a little time to think about it and I'll let you know."

One last plea: if you do nothing else keep trying to understand and connect with your child. The worst thing we can do is get to the point where we decide that the problem is them. Over the years I've had plenty of young people end up in my office who, having made it through their teenage years, have been sent off to therapy by their parents with the message (be it implicit or explicit): fix my child. It's a very familiar dynamic for all youth mental health workers, that the "problem" gets located entirely in the teenager, and the parent's only way to conceptualise what's going on is to then ship their child off to get "fixed".

A word of clarification, because this is an unavoidably emotionally loaded idea: I'm not saying that young people don't develop mental health issues, nor am I saying that the blame should instead be on parents. But if, as a parent, you take yourself out of the equation you are doing your child and indeed yourself a grave disservice. After all, something emotionally challenging has been triggered in you. To place the blame on them and make them "the problem" is to indulge in what we call "project and attack", a way of responding to strong emotions that we'll talk more about later. Suffice it to say, in a relationship, or a family, it is *never* one person's fault. We create dynamics together, and our blind spots — unconscious to us — mean we can unhelpfully disown what is ours and place it on others.

Regulating ourselves, and being flexible, not rigid, enables self-reflection to take place. In general, with any conflict, especially with our children, we should also be asking, "How is what I'm doing contributing to the issue, and how can I do something different that might work better?"

Because we should grow from the experience of parenting as much as our children do.

Parenting and your "significant other" relationship

All parents will know that special joy — and at times the awkward feeling — that comes from recognising yourself in your child. The quirks, the little habits, the preferences and dislikes that mirror us. You are also likely to recognise a fair amount of the other parent in them too, and if you have more than one child you likely feel one is more like you, and one is more like the other parent. Whether this is objectively true is beside the point; it fosters love and attachment. However, it can also fan the flames of the "project and attack" dynamic mentioned above, in that we can see the things we dislike in ourselves in our children and react more strongly to their foibles they have inherited one way or another from us. This gets even more complicated when our children act in ways that are like that of the other parent — and we react in the same helpful or unhelpful ways to those traits.

Even more complicated again is when you are no longer parenting with the other biological parent. It's quite challenging to tolerate and react with love when seeing your child or young person behave in ways that remind you of the person you are no longer in a relationship with — and may even have come to dislike, or worse. But even when we're still in a relationship with the other parent, there are unavoidable things that annoy us or we become impatient with, which then puts the relationship with our child in the firing line.

This is where having another adult around is so helpful, and it doesn't have to be the other parent. Sometimes we need some help to relentlessly hold ourselves to account because there are things about ourselves that we can't see. So, when I talk about the growth that can happen with parenting, this is a very concrete example of what I mean. If we can keep being open, flexible, and reflecting then we not only improve the relationship with our child by reducing the likelihood we end up being dysregulated and rigid, but we also learn more about ourselves, and the impact of our own childhood along the way.

A note on self-reflection, because it is one of those psychobabble terms. To me, reflection is vital in all areas of life, not just parenting. It is that ability to step back and think about our own feelings, thoughts and actions — non-defensively, non-judgementally and ideally with compassion. It's a skill, and like any skill, it can be learned. Therapy develops it, but so does hearing and taking feedback from those we love and trust. *Self*-reflection then is as limited as *self*-help. Ultimately, we need others to learn about us, because we are formed in relationships, and what we need to know most about ourselves can only be found in relationships. And if we rigidly hold the view that our job is to teach our children about themselves, without also recognising that we also learn from them, then we miss out as much as they do.

Growing up and letting go

Many people arrive in therapy together with the ghosts of their parents and their childhood — even if their parents are long gone, or still alive but playing very little part in their life. If our relationship with our parents — or our teens —

has survived adolescence, then we're ready to find ways to relate to our parents as adults, hopefully even as equals. For many, this process unfolds naturally, as it should; however, if the adolescent years have been too rocky and separation hasn't been able to occur, then it will likely remain rocky.

Letting go of children as they grow also means letting go of expectations about how we may want them to be — instead getting to know who they are. The stereotype of the son or daughter that has "disappointed" their parents by failing to achieve, to become a doctor or a lawyer, is too familiar as a stereotype to not reflect aspects of reality. We may all carry aspects of disappointment, whether that be for who we feel our parents wanted us to be, or for the parents we wished we had.

One of the very painful ways that insecure attachment can show up in therapy many years later is the adult who still longs for the wished-for parent. The relationship may still be distinctly unsatisfying, or even abusive, but separation has not occurred, and the parent still impacts in the present. In the adult child lies a wish — what I sometimes call a "memory of the future" — that if they can just get through to the parent, just reach them, help them to change for the better, then the parent that should've been there all along will emerge, and things will be OK. This is the adult version of, "If I just try harder, then they will love me, therefore I am the problem, not them."

It's another form of rigidity, albeit a protective one, where we hold onto the old story because, at an emotional level, the truth is harder and more painful. The truth, that our parent or parents let us down, were flawed human beings, maybe even abjectly neglectful, or explicitly abusive, is painful enough. But letting go of the hope that one day they might change is even more painful, and requires grieving for something that never happened. And once we fully accept the reality, will likely never happen.

This type of grief is one I've seen many times over the years and can also show up amid the very real grief of the parent dying, as it also signals the end of hope for the wished-for change.

Moving away from defensive rigidity, self-blame and accepting our parents — or our children — for who they are, doesn't necessarily make things better, but it does make things honest. When we engage with reality, we can make decisions based on what is then going to help us, rather than continue to hurt us.

Being physically distant can help, and there are many culturally normal ways of doing this, from going away to university, to the great Kiwi tradition of the big OE (Overseas Experience). But physical distance doesn't necessarily create psychological distance, especially if the pain is deep. We all have varying levels of distance and closeness with our own parents, and we are more or less resolved in our relationship with them. There is no perfect, only good enough.

But sadly, for some the distance will grow, and parents may choose to cut off their children, or children their parents. Logically, of course, there are doubtless situations where this is justified. Just because someone is your parent doesn't mean it is possible, or even safe, to have an ongoing relationship with them, and the same in reverse. Cutting off contact in families is still something we don't talk much about, and it occurs more than we might be comfortable admitting. Given what I've said so far about the evolutionary strength of attachment bonds, it should also be clear that I don't think anyone takes such actions lightly. They are decisions always taken from a place of pain, misunderstanding and hurt.

Over the years I've had a number of clients contemplate such actions, and a smaller number take the action. In part, this is because it is hard to do, and in part, because even if you do cut the family member off, you don't solve the problem — not fully. You may protect yourself from the present-day hurt, the current demands or attacks, but you are still left with the legacy. We can't delete the lifelong experience of the person no matter how hard we try. But if the present-day toxicity is such that it hampers our ability to recover from what came before, it can be the only way.

Is it true that adult parents abuse their adult children? Of course. Is it also true that adult children abuse their adult parents? Again, undoubtedly true. But the moral imperative to maintain relationships with parents no matter what is not helpful. Indeed, my cynical view is that the best form of retirement planning is to be a good enough parent so that you ensure your children will want to look after you as you age, not feel that they "should".

SUMMARY

- One of the cornerstones of our emotional health throughout life is the quality of our attachment relationships in our early childhood. Understanding our attachment style can help us understand our adult relationship patterns and the problems we can fall into. Different attachment styles strongly influence how adept we are at regulating our emotions throughout life.

- Validation is the experience of feeling that our views, opinions and thoughts are heard and matter to someone else. For people who grow up in environments that are — on average — not validating (or invalidating) this can leave them struggling to trust and experience their own feelings, and lead to problems with their emotional regulation.

- Children naturally take in what they hear about themselves as they grow up. We all have a "playlist" in our head that is made up of what we heard when we were small. For some this can be loving, for others it can be abusive and critical, and a direct cause of dysregulated emotions.

- Parenting is an exercise in grief and letting go. The task is to allow our children to become who they are, and over time to let them go, without making our feelings, and our struggles with grief, their problems. Flexibility and openness are vital to grief and growth as a parent.

- Parenting teenagers is all about the quality of the relationship, and staying close, even when it's hard and it seems like they don't want you close. Setting boundaries with love and patience is hard and vital — but we can do that in a balanced, flexible manner, rather than in a rigid, authoritarian way.

CHAPTER 3:

Trauma in childhood: Bad things do happen

SO HOW DO SOME PEOPLE end up struggling so much with controlling the volume of their emotional response, while others seem to have no problem getting the volume right?

Well, as we've already covered, we can put some of it down to temperament — how we're born, our early attachment environment and the emotional climate we grow up in. The final factor which we haven't considered in depth is the role of trauma, especially in childhood.

Trauma and dysregulation

Trauma is generally shorthand for Post-Traumatic Stress Disorder, or PTSD, a diagnosis with its history in the initial observations of "shellshocked" soldiers in World War One. As a diagnosis, it somewhat narrowly defines trauma as being exposed to death, threatened death, actual or threatened serious injury, or actual or threatened sexual violence.

However, especially when dealing with developmental trauma, in my view it's always been more useful to listen to oneself when defining what is traumatic, or perhaps better described as overwhelming for us. A more subjective definition of trauma is any event that exceeds our ability to manage our emotional responses, leads to overwhelm and prevents us processing and digesting the memory or experience.

This then highlights a couple of important factors. First, what one person may find traumatic, another may merely find an upsetting event that they manage to cope with. Secondly, the point isn't the trauma, but how we respond emotionally. In other words, our learned or inherited responses to deal with overwhelming distress.

Some of those responses will be formed from environmental factors, some will be the result of temperament. But as we hit life's adversities and find creative — albeit not always constructive — ways to manage, we build up habits that can get further entrenched by subsequent events.

Responses to overwhelming trauma — or symptoms of PTSD — fall into three groups. First, what is called hypervigilance, is essentially chronic anxiety. Our fear response is turned up, and our baseline is set too high. When you think about it, being perpetually on alert because you've experienced trauma makes sense, even though it's pretty unpleasant. This is what I call a "volume knob problem". The volume is too loud on the emotions, they are dysregulated.

Secondly, is what is termed re-experiencing. The more well-known examples are nightmares, flashbacks and intrusive memories — memories of the event that feel as though they come into our mind in ways we can't control. This is also about emotional regulation, but in a less obvious way, which I'll get to below.

And thirdly, numbing. Switching off all feelings by dissociating, losing the thread of the memories or just feeling numb and cut off. Subjectively it's unpleasant, but it also protects us from the pain of the experience — at the cost of being in contact with reality. Numbing becomes a problem when in life more generally we feel like we can't control it happening. Like a mute switch, we have no control over it and it randomly turns on, meaning we can't hear the music even when we want to. Some people experience dissociation as de-realisation, where it can feel as if the world or their experience isn't "real" but instead feels dreamlike or disconnected from reality. Others can feel what we call de-personalisation, as if they aren't themselves, or are no longer in their body. The most extreme form is an out-of-body experience, for some literally floating above their body and looking down at themselves. These seemingly quite extreme or strange experiences make sense when we see them as what people do to tolerate being abused, assaulted or raped. They are all ways to disconnect from the horrifying reality of what is happening to them and survive the experience.

However, not everything that shapes us is traumatic. The emotional atmosphere of a family can shape us without being traumatic — it's all a matter of degree and length of exposure.

The fundamental difference with trauma is that it causes disruptions in memory in ways that other upsetting or difficult experiences don't. That's the re-experiencing bit, essentially if an event is overwhelming enough emotionally speaking, then we are unable to process it. At the risk of mixing my metaphors, think of the memory as food that cannot be digested — and as a result, when the memory is recalled or triggered, it is experienced as if no time has passed. Like emotional indigestion. When these experiences get stuck, then they are re-experienced as if they are happening to us all over again, because the normal processes of memory, forgetting and time distancing us from the event, don't happen.

In that sense, PTSD is as much a problem of memory as it is a problem of anxiety and dysregulation.

It's a common question when people engage in therapy due to traumatic intrusive memories from childhood, to wonder whether they will be able to get rid of their traumatic memories. My answer is that psychotherapy will help turn those intrusive, overwhelming and distressing memories into plain old bad memories. It won't get rid of them because unavoidably those experiences are part of your story, but if they're just bad memories then you will at least have more control over whether you think about them or not.

And what helps to shift them from traumatic memories to bad ones? Increasing our capacity to tolerate and — you guessed it — regulate emotions. Increasing our capacity to tolerate the emotions, means the experience can be digested, and in doing so treated like any other memory. One that loses its power, its intense effect, and over time even fades. Forgetting is also a normal part of our memory system.

What's also important is the protective factors for long-term outcomes in the aftermath of childhood sexual abuse. Now that is not to say there is any "good outcome" — any abuse of children is horrific and damaging. But we do know what sorts of things make it worse, and what tends to result in the long term, severe consequences — leading to a diagnosis of complex PTSD for instance.

The obvious factors are the severity of the abusive act itself, from unwanted touching (least severe) through to penetrative sex and rape (most severe), and the closeness of the relationship with the adult — from a stranger (less severe) to a parent or first-degree relative (most severe). As horrible as it is to think about, to some extent that's just common sense.

The next core factor in determining the severity of long-term consequences relates to the degree of emotion regulation. Please do not read this as any form of victim blaming, but the degree of distress the young person can tolerate — or put it another way the emotion regulation skills they possessed before the incident, and therefore how easily they reach emotional overwhelm is a big factor. As is the amount of support they were able to access at the time. There is, of course, a relationship between these things. It's easy to see that an emotionally validating environment will both equip the young person with more emotional regulation skills, and will be more able to respond helpfully to a traumatic incident. Conversely, a family where abuse is occurring inside the family is unlikely to be particularly emotionally validating. Neither is it a safe place for someone to disclose abuse nor to respond in a validating way even if such a disclosure did occur. In this situation, the factors compound, increasing the risk of long-lasting severe outcomes.

My experience over the years has taught me kids know instinctively if they're safe to disclose abuse. Looking back, it's clear to our adult selves that a disclosure wouldn't have been handled well, even if the person has no recollection of making a conscious choice to not tell anyone. Of course, the dynamics of shame also play a role here, where the understandable response to any kind of abuse is to want to hide it — despite it not being our fault in any way.

So, if we imagine all of this on a slide rule, then it's easy to see that any of these factors being elevated can combine with the others to create situations that are overwhelming and too much to process. It is also easy to see that if the event is distressing enough, then it doesn't matter what skills you bring to the situation, it will likely cause ongoing symptoms.

Now like I said, this is not about victim blaming, nor should it be seen as minimising the impacts of sexual abuse and trauma. But it is a fact that the impacts of childhood abuse do vary from person to person, and that some might be left with ongoing traumatic symptoms for years, while others can recover and process it as a very unpleasant memory.

As complicated as that all might seem, it's important because one of the ways that we can get ourselves into trouble with our thinking around the impact of distressing events is to engage in what I call the "Suffering Olympics".

It's human nature to compare our situations, trauma and struggles with others. This can even be helpful, but often it isn't. One of the common ways to self-invalidate is to look to those whom we assess as having had it "worse" than us, however, we might define that. We then self-invalidate, define the other as doing better than us and use this as a stick to further beat ourselves with.

Understanding the complex interplay of factors that are involved with how events impact us is important to challenge the Suffering Olympics. In doing so we can see that we did the best we could with what we had at the time, and our only task is to find ways to overcome the challenges we've been dealt.

When we truly come from a place of validation the impact itself is the evidence of the severity — we don't have to justify the feelings or the symptoms. Logically, if we are deeply distressed and traumatised then what happened to us was deeply hurtful and traumatising. The proof is in the feelings.

When it comes to recovery, the good news is, anything we do to help ourselves better regulate our emotional responses and more consciously control what we pay attention to, will help.

What can be hard though, is the first steps. Understandably, people who have experienced a lot of trauma and distress work very hard to avoid their emotions, and as a result their internal experiences. This can look — and feel — like they are lurching from control and rigidity to overwhelming explosions of emotions and distress. This is because we can only keep the lid on emotions for so long before they overflow in ways that can seem at times quite confusing.

This is what I call the "straw that broke the camel's back" problem.

"Trigger" is another one of those words that has been overused to the point where it hardly has any useful meaning any more. It has come to mean anything that causes people to get upset — and while the idea of "trigger warnings" are well-intentioned, it has diluted the meaning. I much prefer the more recent version of "Content Warning".

Technically a "trigger" in trauma terms, is anything that causes the person to recall or re-experience a past traumatic experience. Having someone standing over you and yelling may trigger memories of an angry, abusive parent, for instance. Or the war veteran who dives under the table when hearing fireworks going off.

Often triggers are that literal and easy to understand. But with the straw that broke the camel's back problem, it is a lot less obvious. When emotional distress generally gets too high, it can seem like the smallest thing can tip us into overwhelm. This can be very hard to understand, for the person who is overwhelmed, and even more so for those around them. It can lead to the problem of unintentional invalidation, because, well frankly, it can look "crazy" if you don't understand what's going on.

But it does also highlight one of the golden rules, not just of therapy, but also emotions generally: there is no *wrong* way to feel.

Every emotion we have makes sense, it just may not be immediately apparent at the moment. But if we start from the place of validation, and assume it's happened for a reason, then the general response, to ourselves and others is one of curiosity and acceptance.

And I don't use the word "crazy" lightly. I think the difference between feelings that we can make sense of, and being overcome by feelings that make no sense, is that the latter subjectively feels like going crazy. It's also the natural outcome of abuse, neglect and invalidation.

Neglect

Of course, trauma isn't always obvious. And the less obvious it is, the more difficult it can be to understand, validate and make part of our story. Normally when we think of trauma we think of "bad things happening", which is technically called trauma of commission. But there is also trauma of omission or "necessary things didn't happen". More commonly we call this neglect.

It's not unusual for people to arrive in therapy with little clear knowledge of the extent of their neglect, especially if all their material needs were met, and the "omission" was in the form of emotional connection, love, support and validation.

We all only know what we know. And what we know is what we consider to be normal. Emotional neglect can take many forms, and most of them aren't deliberately malicious. As we discussed in the last chapter, parents generally are doing the best they can with what they have, given their own experiences of childhood.

Nonetheless, neglect lowers our expectations — it leaves us expecting what we know. It also can feel like trying to catch smoke when you first become aware of it. It can often be behind a difficulty accepting or feeling comfortable with closeness, kindness, or simply accepting compliments. And in the absence of what we need, most of us develop negative ideas about ourselves to explain the fact that we feel unloved, unappreciated or generally not cherished.

Some research suggests that trauma of omission can be worse and more long-lasting than the trauma of commission. I think this buys into the "Suffering Olympics" a bit too much — however, it certainly emphasises that neglect is more impactful than we might think. While research is useful, in terms of therapy and recovery from trauma the most important part is having a story of your life, who you are, and why you respond to things the way you do. That is validating and makes sense.

A story that makes you feel not crazy. Because when we can develop that for ourselves, it is inherently validating. It isn't about what label you have or what skill you need to learn to help manage your emotions, it's about believing in a felt way that what happened to you explains the struggles you face, and in understanding this, you will also overcome them.

When therapists make these kinds of links between how you feel now, and what your emotional development was, we call this an "interpretation". We don't call it the "truth", it's more a hypothesis, an idea to try on for size to see if it fits. When we develop a more detailed story about how we came to be the way we are, then we call it a "formulation".

It takes time for new stories to be woven, and for new understandings to build. And each person's story, and the way it impacted them, is unique. But shining a light on these connections and patterns is a very straightforward way to understand the somewhat mysterious process that therapists talk about as making the unconscious, conscious.

Why fear sticks

PTSD is technically an anxiety disorder, and while I hopefully have conveyed that trauma, abuse and neglect are more complicated than just anxiety, an understandable fear response is at the heart of it.

Fear as an emotion is often seen as one of the most universal across all species, being one of the four "F's" of instinctual behaviour — feeding, fighting, fleeing and sexual behaviour. In evolutionary terms, these all increase the chances of survival, and so have been selected for across many generations, in all species, including ours.

It's pretty self-explanatory how fears serve to keep us alive, but a few things are important to map out in a bit more detail before we consider anxiety. First, there is always a wide variability in any population for any trait, that's how genetics work and is the raw material for evolution. So, with regards to fear, there are people who like to rock climb with no ropes, all the way through to people who prefer to stay home most of the time and take no risks in their life — and everything in between. At the same time, at a population level, it's always a balancing act. On the one hand, it makes sense that we might tend towards being fearful to survive. However, it's also true that we need adventurous people. It benefits their survival to strike out and find new populations to breed with and discover new ways of doing things that also benefit their survival.

In short: too much fearlessness increases the chances of being dead. Too little decreases the chances of venturing into the world and breeding. Massively oversimplified, I know, but think big-picture evolution here.

Secondly, it makes sense that fear is easily learnt, and generalised. What do we mean by generalised? Well, let's thrash the evolutionary trope a little more and imagine one of our hominid ancestors stumbles across a sabre-tooth tiger, is attacked, runs away and survives. It makes sense for that fear to not only be very quickly learned but also generalised to include all sabre-tooth tigers, not just the one that attacked him. It might even be expanded to a generalised fear of all tiger-like creatures: large four-legged creatures for example. It certainly isn't easily forgotten. Even if he never saw another sabre-toothed tiger for the rest of his life, our ancestor would likely remain fearful of them until he died.

Thirdly, our imagined ancestor then tells his wider

community in great detail about his encounter, and through story, imagination and relationships generates helpful fear in others who have never seen a sabre-tooth tiger. Those who he regales with his story, might feel anxiety — if we strictly define anxiety as fear in the absence of fearful stimuli.

So, we see anxiety requires imagination and is by its very nature about being fearful of things that haven't happened yet. Its sensitivity is its strength, at least in survival terms, but also its biggest weakness, and helps to explain why we as a species are prone to anxiety — even as our day-to-day life continues to get safer — on average, at least in the so-called developed world. Recent research suggests that despite this absolute safety, anxiety has overtaken depression as the most common mental health disorder globally. We are both, on average, safer *and* more anxious.

The recent Covid-19 pandemic provides an interesting case study in the population-level dynamics of fear and valid anxiety. Putting aside the complications of the anti-vaccination movements, and outright denialists, for the majority that largely followed the rules, it's been an anxious couple of years.

Here in Aotearoa, we learnt about the virus from a distance and acted based on a very real anxiety. We took universal actions — staying home to protect ourselves and each other. The arrival of cases and the ongoing spread of the virus heightened everyone's anxiety because we're very quick to learn anxiety. Then, as we made our way through the stage where we had eliminated the virus, it was still hard for many to venture back out and be around other people in public. Anxiety is hard to unlearn.

Once we had a vaccine, the resulting waves of infection kept coming. We now had to learn to manage an endemic spread and it became even more difficult to figure out how anxious to be — and so individual responses started to vary, and of course cause conflict.

This is the nuance that is so hard with the reality of anxiety. Sabre-tooth tigers are simple to risk assess — the reality of life? An invisible pathogen? Not so much.

What really causes problems with anxiety isn't the emotion itself, even though it's pretty uncomfortable, especially if it reaches the intensity of panic. However, the practical problems of anxiety can all be traced back to the main behaviour it motivates — avoidance.

Covid-19 lockdowns harnessed the desire to run and hide, as it facilitated safety and compliance, at least in the short term: fear-motivated avoidance can be a great short-term response. But chronic dysregulated anxiety — fear in the absence of anything to fear — leads to avoidance of imagined situations, regardless of whether they pose a threat. Of course, it's rarely that black and white., Even more complicated is fear that is out of proportion to the actual threat. Fear is valid, but the volume is turned up too high.

And because we've avoided the threat, and used our imagination to create a fearful scenario, we never get to potentially unlearn the fear by testing it in the reality of the real-world situation. We only have our imagination to rely on.

Over time, anxiety reinforces itself via the behaviour of avoidance, if we let it.

Of course, temperament also plays a role, some people are more sensitive to anxiety, and more emotionally sensitive generally. It can be a good idea to get a handle on whether you're someone who tends to respond quickly to a threat, and/or has trouble unlearning it. Some people tend to over-generalise, hence one of the anxiety diagnoses being "Generalised Anxiety Disorder".

In general, though, avoidance is the enemy and gradually learning how to tolerate anxiety long enough to unlearn it is the key. But we absolutely need other people for this process to work, not just to (perhaps quite literally) hold our hand, or support us after we've done something hard. We also need others to help us accurately judge the risks of things. We all need each other to help us reality-check our anxieties. Anxiety self-help is hard because it requires us to make that assessment of things we're anxious about, which by their very nature will seem frightening.

When we pool our perspectives, on average we do much better. Some people will have encouraging stories they can relate about their experiences with anxiety — public speaking for example. In fact, a number of studies have shown some people fear public speaking more than death. This says something about how good we are, on average, at managing existential fear, and how much of a herd animal we truly are. With public speaking, it's the humiliation that drives the fear: the ultimate social death.

Some people love public speaking. Some will refuse to ever do it. And most of us figure out how to do it despite feeling anxious. We talk with people, share strategies, attend Toastmasters, or more generally embrace it as a skill to learn and grab opportunities out of a desire to change.

Some have a tendency towards avoidance, and some run — or at least walk thoughtfully — towards anxiety.

Either way, if we can accurately assess risk, make a conscious decision to walk towards what we fear, and stay open and flexible enough for our mind to learn — or more accurately unlearn — the anxiety, then we build mastery. Over time we can respond flexibly to things that cause that response. In general, we call this exposure, and more detailed gradual exposure therapies are a very helpful and successful approach to an anxiety disorder.

Of course, avoidance imposes its own consequences and is one of the key diagnostic criteria of an anxiety disorder. People struggle to attend or engage in things because of their anxiety, and in becoming aware of that try to change it.

I've wondered more and more recently if this is one of the ways that technology is unhelpful. It became apparent during the lockdowns of 2020 and 2021, that many of us could conduct our lives (personal and professional), shop and entertain ourselves completely via the internet. Avoidance of the wider world is now possible, if not entirely desirable. It was certainly useful during lockdowns, however.

For the first time, I conducted all my therapy sessions online for an extended period through the various lockdowns. Despite generally being a fan of technology, I'd always resisted online therapy, as it seemed like a diluted experience. However, it was certainly preferable to nothing, and at least we were all in it together, trying to tolerate this new, required way of relating as a community. But outside of that necessity, I prefer face-to-face. I've read various ideas and research about why it isn't as good and there isn't a clear consensus yet. But my experience is that something is missing.

Maybe it is just me. I do wonder whether the next generation will notice less difference than I do, but there are so many unconscious and subconscious communications happening that we just can't detect in the same way online, I doubt it will ever truly feel the same. I did find it easier with people I knew well, and clients I had seen for a longer period. But I largely didn't meet with new clients because I just couldn't find a way to make that ever-so-vital initial connection in quite the same way.

So at least in theory, tackling avoidance is straightforward — target it, be deliberate, get support and do it gradually. But what happens if what you're avoiding isn't a place, an activity, or a thing. What if what you're afraid of is inside you?

Fear of fear

We don't just have emotional responses to things outside us. PTSD is a fear of re-experiencing the trauma, which replays inside us. Panic attacks are the fear of fear. The panic feeling is so intense it is traumatising in and of itself, and so the merest whiff of that feeling and we start to panic, setting off a hair-trigger cascading response which for people who have ever experienced it is so awful you genuinely feel like you're going to die.

In extreme states of dysregulation, we can also become sensitised and fearful of other emotional states and internal experiences. We can come to fear ourselves or at least our internal world.

This internal landscape of emotions and responses is something that psychotherapy is particularly good at helping people unpick, learn about and change. In particular, it can be helpful to start to notice what we call secondary emotions. Specifically, these are the emotions we have in response to another emotion. For example, fear of fear. Or guilty about feeling angry. Or ashamed of desire.

We all tend to have emotions that we're prone to, and the problem with a secondary emotion is they can be self-perpetuating. Once they've got away on us, they can keep on triggering themselves, independent of the primary emotion, and the situation that prompted that feeling.

Avoidance is much trickier of course, but we all avoid our internal experiences in one way or another. Mindfulness is so popular because we all increasingly tend towards avoidance of our internal experience. It seems to be a bit of a modern problem. But when we keep trying to avoid painful internal states, we can often end up replaying the very invalidation, abuse or attacks that led to the problem in the first place. And because we can't ever get away from ourselves, we can also tend towards more intense kinds of avoidance to try and keep the unwanted emotions away. Drugs and alcohol often become a go-to — a reliable form of numbing, at least for a while. Working long hours, avoiding intimacy, and becoming overly obsessed with exercise can at first glance seem less problematic, but they also take their toll.

When psychotherapists talk about an internalised abuser or persecutor, or maybe a self-critic, this is what that little piece of psychobabble means. That part of us responds to ourselves and our feelings in ways that make us feel bad, and keeps us feeling bad.

Generalised, this can lead to a particular kind of anxiety, where we become terrified to feel and avoidant of life. Numb, limited and cut-off but occasionally prone to overwhelming waves of emotion because we've painted ourselves into a corner, and are unable to avoid the feelings forever. I've seen people come out of chronic addictions feeling like this, drowning in the feelings. That's often where good residential treatment programmes come in.

Mindfulness can indeed help, but for this particular struggle, therapy works best. Trying to meditate from this heightened emotional place can simply overwhelm people and tip them into more escalating distress. Therapy helps in this situation. Gradually through talking, noting and describing, you get used to just being with yourself, in the presence of another — safe and consistent — human being. For some people, this *is* the therapy. Just being able to talk, feel and experience. No clever tricks, techniques or worksheets. Just finding ways to compassionately engage with oneself and learn over time we don't need to fear ourselves, our emotions or our memories. We can bear it, without falling apart — as long as we're not alone.

Technically, what I'm describing is graduated exposure to internal states, but it's easier to ask people to sit down, get comfortable and just try to say whatever comes to mind. Even though saying whatever comes to mind is frequently not comfortable.

On meds

It's not possible to talk about trauma, anxiety and distress without considering medication, but I do so reluctantly. Not because I'm anti-medications for diagnosed mental health disorders, but because it's complicated. It can be too easy to get labelled as falling on one side or other of the medication debate.

Let me be clear about a couple of things. First, I'm not a medical doctor, and not trained in psychiatric medication and its prescribing. Secondly, I'm fundamentally a pragmatist. I'm a fan of whatever works and there is no doubt in my mind that medication such as the modern anti-depressant medications — Selective Serotonin Reuptake Inhibitors or SSRIs — like Prozac and Citalopram, work for many people.

It's also true that many people absolutely need regular anti-psychotic medications to keep the intense, disturbing and dysregulated experiences of a psychotic illness under control enough to live a structured and satisfying life. I am all for what works.

It's also true that medications don't always work. Or don't work as well as some might be led to believe. Or don't work as much as people might want them to. And it's also true that the growing domination of a medical model of psychiatric illness has limited the range of treatments available for people struggling with emotional distress. By promoting itself as the only panacea, the medical model has pushed psychotherapy in all its forms to the sidelines — largely for reasons of cost. Systems will seek to treat people for the least possible cost, I accept that. And there is little doubt that medication is a reasonable place to start with severe mental health struggles and is often helpful. But the growth of depression and anxiety has seen a rise in the use of medications, and with so-called mild to moderate depression and anxiety, the evidence is less compelling.

In general, if your symptoms are severe enough to warrant medication, then ideally you should be in some kind of talk therapy too. The evidence for depression is that therapy and medication are more effective together than on their own. And while there are many practical reasons why this isn't always possible, you will still find prescribing clinicians who will tell you that all you need is medication. This is simply false.

If you're reading this and you're taking medication, don't stop without talking to your prescriber. But do consider using the medication to support you to make the changes you want in your life and take credit for the work you're doing. Regardless of whether you're in therapy or not, it's you doing the changing, not the pills.

SUMMARY

- Trauma can be defined as anything that happens to us that overwhelms our capacity to cope emotionally. Trauma doesn't necessarily cause ongoing problems, but when it does it is a problem of memory and can cause disruptions in our emotion regulation system, especially when the trauma occurs in childhood.

- Neglect can be seen as "trauma of omission" or trauma that is caused by necessary emotional needs not being met in childhood. Although harder to define — we don't know what we don't know — it can be just as damaging.

- Fear is an understandable response to trauma, our fear system is incredibly powerful, sensitive and teaching us to be afraid of things that can hurt us is its job. This can cause problems if it teaches us to be afraid of other human beings, even more so, those who are close to us.

- Trauma disrupts our fear systems and can cause ongoing problems with anxiety. It can also cause fear of emotions, as we struggle with difficult, overwhelming trauma-related emotions and become understandably fearful of feeling that way. Responding rigidly to our emotional states is an attempt at safety that ultimately backfires.

- The aim when dealing with trauma is to turn traumatic memories and experiences into plain-old bad memories. This requires a trusting relationship and increasing our capacity to feel the emotions that come along with the memory. Digesting the experience doesn't make it go away, but we can live more easily with something when it is "just" a bad memory.

CHAPTER 4:
Depression and low mood

A PARTICULAR STUDY FROM my undergraduate psychology days has always stuck with me. In short, it is believed that people who are depressed perceive reality more accurately — which when I first heard it seemed rather shocking to me. Does this mean that a pervasively negative view of the world is the "correct" one? At first glance, it can seem this way.

Much the same thing can of course be said about anxiety, and it would seem increasingly so in recent times. Climate change, pandemics, armed conflict in Europe — there is no shortage of things to be fearful about.

So why aren't we all depressed, nervous wrecks? Well ...

Back to the study. Firstly, the "effect" found in the research has a lovely name: "depressive realism". And it has held up as a theory since the late 1970s, so it's a "thing" — at least in the Western populations where it's been studied. As an idea it has a common-sense appeal, especially to cynics, who are prone to proclaim themselves as not cynics but realists. But it also has some implications for many widely held ideas about how to be happier and, well, less depressed.

The first and biggest implication is that those who *aren't* in the grips of depression are the ones who are, ever so subtly, deluded. They're the ones misperceiving reality. Or are they?

In contrast to this depressingly realistic study (or is it realistically depressing) is the idea that human beings have what is termed a "negativity bias". This is to say that our natural set point is slightly negative, which when you think about makes sense from a survival point of view.

If you were designing a mood system of human beings, it makes complete sense that to feel happy is an optimistic delusion — and that from the point of view of staying alive, being slightly negative works in our favour because it means we're more likely to avoid danger, overestimate threats and generally treat the world as a slightly dangerous place. From a purely evolutionary perspective, this works out in the long term.

While these two theories might seem at first glance in contradiction to one another, I don't see it that way. I think it is true that life for most of humanity's history, and for most species on earth is — in the words of philosopher Thomas Hobbs — "nasty, brutish and short". As a result, human beings tend naturally towards the negative, because that is generally true, and as a result, our mood system is generally pulling us in that direction.

When we're talking about a "mood system" we're really talking about beliefs, expectations and filters — that filter and colour the world, and how we see and perceive it. What our brain does to the facts. And there's little argument that wearing slightly rose-tinted glasses makes the mortal roller coaster that much more pleasant to be on. But to don those glasses requires work — both against reality and against our natural tendencies.

Of course, the other big implication is for how we commonly think about depression. A lot of (generally misapplied, or at least out of context) uses of Cognitive Behavioural Therapy or "CBT" focus on changing your beliefs that lead to depressive feelings. Change what you feel, by changing the way you think. Some of the CBT tools teach people to look for evidence for their negative views and to challenge them. This can be very useful and makes sense if we just consider the negativity bias. But if what you believe is actually in line with reality, then this can be a problem.

For instance, let's take the idea that you don't matter. Well, it's pretty much true for all of us. We're all replaceable, and in the grand scheme of an infinite universe, where billions of people are alive right now, what's one more, give or take. It can be a miserable thought if you dwell on it. (Please don't.)

But I believe the problem really is a search for what is TRUE. You can always make facts, numbers and a wide view of reality look miserable and unappealing. That's easy.

The trick is not to not look for what is TRUE but instead to consider what WORKS.

What particular delusion, filter or idea helps here? If a feeling that you don't matter is the problem — find situations that generate that feeling for you, generally relationships and connections. Find people (or pets) to whom you matter. I believe this is pretty much the whole reason dogs work as pets, and for many, act as mental health support. It's very obvious you matter to a dog — and I say this as a cat person, which I understand is a particular pathology of its own — because dogs are pathologically needy. They excel at needing you. Whether or not you matter factually is easily soothed by obviously mattering to someone or something.

You likely have people you matter to, and that matter to you. You likely also have things that are meaningful to you, and maybe even only to you.

Because again, that's the point. We can all get lost in the meaninglessness of it all, another common "depressive realism" problem. Again, the point isn't whether or not existence is inherently meaningful, what matters is what works — finding meaning specifically in your day-to-day life.

There is a playfulness to all of this, and a flexibility that one needs to foster, however. I talk more about the problems of rigidity in following chapters, but it is an understandable response to fear, trauma and uncertainty. To close down, to look for certainty and predictability. To stick to what we know. The problem is that that thinking tends to lead to more depressive realism, and in doing so decreases our general openness, creativity and ability to hold "reality" lightly.

What works is to be open to multiple perspectives and ways of seeing things, and in doing so, to flexibly try things and as much as possible do what works in each situation.

The problem with too much self-esteem

So how does depressive realism impact self-esteem? Well in part it tells us it's also possible to overshoot into unhelpful optimism or what some have more recently dubbed toxic positivity. At face value, it is reasonable to want to feel better about oneself, more confident, and like a better person. But better than what, or who?

Throughout the 1970s and '80 self-esteem was lauded as the key to life success. It was a very fashionable idea and persists in most ideas about self-improvement and wellbeing.

But what does it mean, to have esteem in oneself? It means two things that can be particularly problematic. First, it means being better than others. It is inherently competitive and by raising oneself up, you also inevitably put yourself above others. In that respect, it's a very Western-capitalist idea, inherently selfish and individualistic in its foundations.

Secondly, it's also conditional. Your feelings of esteem are reliant upon doing well, being good or successful. Your worth is not inherent; it relies on success and ability.

The most ridiculous outcome of this self-esteem

movement was participation prizes; the idea that there are no winners or losers, and everyone gets a prize because, it was thought, albeit with the best of intentions, that failing or losing would damage a child's self-esteem. (The reality of this is much more complicated of course and misunderstands child development and individual differences in its application.) For what it's worth, a better approach is to not focus on prizes at all when kids are young, but rather to focus on participation and having fun. Too much competition too early can stifle openness to making mistakes which is vital to learning. Early on, learning and having fun is the prize — it's intrinsically rewarding — we don't need to add participation prizes to the mix at all!

Self-esteem doesn't give us wriggle room to be ourselves, in all its messy brilliance. It's like the unforgiving boss who only accepts perfection and a good mood. It doesn't teach us how to fail, it doesn't allow for mistakes and simply being a fallible human. Much more useful as a concept is self-compassion.

Self-compassion is the belief that we are worthy of love and care, just because we are alive. It is the idea that even in our failures we can be kind and learn from our mistakes. Where self-esteem is achievement-focussed and conditional, self-compassion is unconditional and forgiving.

Self-compassion lives in the real world and allows for differences because we all have different strengths and weaknesses. It allows for sadness, pain and failure in the understanding that these feelings are part of being human. It encourages us to always treat ourselves with respect, and ultimately to be our own best friend in our attitude and our behaviour.

Growing self-compassion requires practice and patience. It also requires a full acceptance of, and engagement with, the present moment and ourselves.

Affirmations

Related to the ideas around self-esteem, is the idea that we just need to repeatedly tell ourselves positive things. You know, positive affirmations.

But what does it mean to "use positive affirmations"?

The cliché is standing in front of the mirror every morning and saying ten times, "I'M A GOOD PERSON!" More generally it is intentionally telling yourself positive things about yourself, with the aim of feeling better and eventually believing them to be true.

As an idea it's certainly appealing; perhaps that's why it's been so popular. Just convince yourself to think something positive and things change! It may be appealing, but it is wrong. In fact, in some cases it may be dangerous.

If you already have pretty good self-esteem and mental health, then affirmations don't make much difference. They might give you a temporary feel-good boost, but they certainly don't do any harm.

However, if you suffer from depression or anxiety, have low self-esteem or hold negative ideas about yourself they can make you feel worse, and deepen depression.

Positive affirmations fail in two important ways.

First, if you have negative ideas about yourself, then telling yourself the opposite causes internal conflict that actually makes you feel worse. Many studies have shown that when people with low self-esteem repeat positive statements to themselves, they feel more depressed — not less.

Secondly, if positive affirmations don't match reality, they can set people up to fail. To repeatedly try to tell yourself that you will succeed at everything you try, that you are talented, that you will get that dream job, doesn't help if you have — in reality — little chance of success.

In short, positive affirmations can be another form of invalidation that doesn't match how we feel and leaves us feeling more like the person we're trying to change.

Changing behaviour takes work, and it takes time. You can't create happiness or calm via an Instagram meme. The idea that change can be achieved through something as simple as inspiring ideas, positive thinking or seeing something from a different point of view, seems absurdly reductive.

Therapy is about engaging with reality, learning to live with all life throws at us, and learning to not run away from the painful bits, even though it's human nature to do so.

As inconvenient as it might be, real change comes from hard work, from allowing ourselves to fully feel and live with what is, and so much of what is often represented by the self-help, inspiring quote culture is shallow and devoid of reality: junk food for the soul. An emotional sugar hit.

So, when we consider self-esteem, positive affirmations and feel-good culture against depressive realism it becomes clear that getting the balance right is important. And just telling ourselves we're great is nowhere near as effective as being more generally loving and doing things that lead to the feelings we want.

The myth of self-sabotage

But what do we do if our feelings lead us down dark paths, acting in ways that may be destructive or simply don't work?

First, let's consider self-sabotage.

The idea we can do things to sabotage ourselves is one of those concepts that also has much common-sense appeal. Yet what are we saying when we describe ourselves — or other people — as being self-destructive?

Most often it's a throwaway line, "I don't know why I did it, I guess I'm just self-destructive!" or "You're your own worst enemy!" And without a doubt, many things we do that may not make much sense to us can seem that way.

Drinking or taking drugs to excess, deliberately hurting ourselves, arguing with and hurting those we love, infidelity, avoiding important meetings or even job interviews, all can make it look like we are our own worst enemy.

The problem when we just shrug our shoulders and resign ourselves to being "self-sabotaging" is it doesn't help us to understand ourselves. In fact, it can leave us feeling that it's something we can't change.

Like any behaviour, if you look closely enough, even the most self-attacking behaviours can be understood, and if we can understand them, we can also change them.

Take self-harm for example. It seems to be a clear, deliberate effort to cause ourselves pain by attacking our own bodies and causing injury.

But when it comes to intent, quite the opposite is true: self-harm is an attempt to manage intense emotional pain. It is a form of intense distraction that hacks our biology to shock our attention away from painful thoughts and emotions. Physical pain is the price of ridding oneself of the emotions. It can actually be seen as an attempt — albeit dangerous — to make things better.

The key, when we try to make sense of these things, is not whether they are a deliberate effort to hurt ourselves, but what is the short-term payoff? Because that's what makes them "work".

Seen from this point of view, all these behaviours make perfect sense. They are either an attempt to cope with painful emotions or overwhelming tension or a way to avoid them.

We bail out of the job interview because the performance anxiety is overwhelming, and we fear failure: avoidance offers short-term relief. We drink or use drugs to escape distress and tension, even though the long-term costs — hangovers, health problems, addiction — all outweigh the short-term relief.

We do this because it is human nature to favour short-term relief, and no more so than for people who, for whatever reason, are in the grip of overwhelming distress.

We all make seemingly "bad" decisions when the future ceases to exist or has disappeared from view.

Drugs and addiction

Addictions to alcohol and other drugs is a special category of the short-term relief problem of course, with one very unhelpful twist — addictions are treated like a moral failing, a weakness or an indulgence. It adds a layer of judgement to the self-sabotage fallacy, and in doing so an extra level of stigma.

When we look past the moral judgment, much of what the evidence tells us about drug addiction flies in the face of many commonly held ideas.

For instance, the fact that most people change their use of all drugs — including so-called "hard drugs" like methamphetamine and heroin — with no assistance.

Or that not everyone who uses illegal drugs causes harm to themselves or others.

Or that the most dangerous drug, and the only one where the withdrawal can kill you — isn't heroin. It's alcohol.

Or that the way we currently criminalise — or don't — various drugs bears no resemblance to their level of danger or potential for dependence.

Alcohol, by any measure of risks, is the most dangerous — and not because it's consumed the most. It's the most harmful to our health, one of the most dependence-creating, and causes wider harm to others, but is legal and very lightly regulated.

On the other hand, the psychedelic drug LSD — while not without potential for harm — is non-addictive and for most users causes little harm, but is "Class A" in Aotearoa, meaning it is classified as having a very high potential for harm. This classification also means its legitimate uses haven't been able to be researched for over 50 years. Yes, for a small portion of the population, it can trigger an underlying psychosis, and that should not be minimised, but so can cannabis, and even alcohol can trigger psychosis.

The moral view is not without any basis in fact. Alcohol and drugs do cause harm. But moralising, focussing on the individual as either the failure or without any will to forgo their chemical of choice leads to punishment and punitive measures, like prohibition and the criminalising of users.

The ultimate enactment of the self-sabotage approach, or more accurately sabotage of another.

In my many years of treating people who struggle with their use of alcohol or other drugs, as well as being a person who has at times had more than a passing interest in drug culture, one thing is clear to me — some people use alcohol and drugs with little consequence to themselves or others, while for others the use ruins their lives. They're not mutually exclusive groups by any means, one can move from one to the other, usually from the "no problem" group to the "ruin your life" group, but also in the other direction.

And the factor that gets people into trouble is, roughly speaking, how much pain you're trying to manage. This makes sense when you understand some of the basic mechanisms of reward and reinforcement. We use drugs, from caffeine to nicotine, alcohol, stimulants, depressants and psychedelic drugs because they make us feel good — or at the very least, feel different. That short-term reward is highly reinforcing — and connecting any short-term effect to longer-term impacts is a difficult problem for human beings generally. As the old saying goes, "the problem with smoking is that one cigarette never killed anybody".

In simplistic terms, if we start from a place of generally

feeling OK, and then use a drug, the gap between how we felt, and we feel after using it, is not huge. But if we are generally in a state of tension, anxiety, misery or fear then the gap between how we felt before and after using the drug is bigger. The removal of pain is at least as rewarding as the creation of pleasure. So, for people in a lot of distress, the reinforcement effect of a mood-altering substance is subjectively larger.

There are of course non-harmful ways to feel better or remove pain, and if they don't cause harm, we generally don't refer to these things as an addiction — with some exceptions.

The medium to long-term harm is the real issue. Which again in simple terms is the health impacts, and the subjective experience of feeling addicted, or needing more of the substance over time to achieve the desired state, feeling less control over the decision to use, and the use having negative consequences on one's life.

In psychological terms, over time other ways of managing emotional tension fall away and we become increasingly reliant on the substance to manage our emotional responses. It's also true that a point of no return happens where the solution (alcohol for instance) becomes the problem, while also being the solution. We feel miserable because of our drinking and the consequences of our drinking, and at the same time turn to alcohol to try and feel better.

And when we make the definition of trauma wide and allow for all sorts of experiences in our past that can cause distress, this way of viewing addictions makes a lot of sense. Researchers into trauma have codified what they call an "Adverse Childhood Experience" score or ACE (see page 82), as a way to try and quantify the impacts of chronic childhood trauma, and how it balances up against what the research categorises as protective factors.

The relationship between trauma and addictions is clear. People who have had one Adverse Childhood Event are two to four times more likely to start using alcohol or drugs at an early age (a clear risk factor for addiction) compared to those without an ACE score. People with an ACE score of 5 or higher are up to ten times more likely to experience addiction compared with people who haven't experienced childhood trauma.

Other factors are at play of course: culture, exposure or access to alcohol and drugs, and variability in what particular chemical people prefer at an individual level. It is also true that not all people who experience ACEs are doomed to become addicts, but it is a clear and high risk — and not just for addiction. Rates of mental health diagnoses (of course) and preventable physical health conditions are also similarly higher.

In short, morality or character has nothing to do with it. People who fall into addiction are simply doing the best they can with what they have. Just like the rest of us. Locking them up and throwing away the key achieves nothing but more pain and misery for people likely to have already had their fair share of both.

The reality of depression

None of what we've discussed so far should in any way minimise the very real and debilitating reality of depression for those who suffer with a diagnosable depressive illness. The experience of a major depressive episode is debilitating, can feel deeply inescapable, and for some can be deadly. Experienced as an unrelenting sadness, self-attack, or an absence of feeling — a painful numbing — in its most severe form, it can leave people unable to move, function or look after themselves. In its slightly less-debilitating forms, it leaves people feeling like life has lost all its joy, colour and meaning. And it generally leads to a withdrawal

— from connection with the things we love, but more problematically, the people we love, and who love us.

Depression destroys connections by leaving us feeling that even love doesn't matter. Some say it is the opposite of love, and it is certainly its enemy.

Depression is also the most impacted by what I've described previously as "concept creep". It has become a description of emotion, which is an understandable, albeit at times problematic consequence of us generally becoming more familiar with psychological terms and diagnoses.

While depression isn't really a "feeling" — I'm not sure it's helpful to describe ourselves as a "bit depressed today" — it does, however, exist on a continuum. Recent public conversations have talked about what is now called "mild to moderate" mental health problems, largely depression and anxiety. With depression, it is true that outside of the psychiatric diagnosis of Major Depressive Episode, people can also struggle with Dysthymic Disorder, a chronic low mood that interferes with day-to-day life, but where people often can keep trudging along, perhaps even hiding the extent of their distress from workmates, and friends. Some describe this as "quiet depression", but whatever we call it, it can be equally debilitating — and for some it can slide into a more severe acute depression.

There are of course a million theories about why depression is increasingly prevalent, from the weird and wonderful through to the hard science — but the reality is for any individual case we don't necessarily know for sure. To be presented with a set of variables and make an accurate prediction as to whether someone is going to develop depression in the future is hit and miss. As we've talked about, if you've experienced previous traumatic events, especially in childhood — what the research calls "Adverse Childhood Experiences" or ACEs — it is possible to predict you will be at a higher risk of some kind of mental health struggle, but not necessarily what specific type.

In addition to trauma, we do know the sorts of things that make people more vulnerable to developing depression. Some physical conditions can mimic depression, thyroid imbalances for example.

When it comes to psychological risk factors, they include family history, in part reflecting possible genetic links. Another risk factor is the thinking styles or behaviours developed in childhood, in particular negative thinking styles. Low or poor self-image leads to a tendency to self-blame, as do high levels of self-criticism. Childbirth and other major life transitions are also potential factors, especially if there is also a family history of mood disorders. Other risk factors include physical injury or disability, and major losses.

Grief is the natural experience that at face value most looks like depression, and for some grief can morph into depression. It can be hard to pick the difference sometimes, and increasingly psychiatry can blur this line even further, especially by prescribing anti-depressant medications for what we might consider normal grief. In my experience, the difference is subjective, but easy to track once you know what to look for.

Grief moves and changes over time. Depression can look like grief but gets stuck or stagnates. The normal ebb and flow of grief is intense and acute. As time passes the pain doesn't lessen initially, at least when you're feeling it, but the amount of time you feel it lessens, and the gaps of time between when you get hit by a wave of grief grows longer. Time is what is required, to readjust our attachment system, to re-learn that the person we value — be it a deceased parent, the tragic death of a friend, or a relationship break up — is no longer around.

For time to work its magic and for the natural flow and

process of grief to happen, we also need to give it space. We need to allow ourselves to feel it. Working hard to not feel it via avoidance behaviours like working harder, drinking or using drugs just prolongs the process, and can lead to getting stuck — and depression.

We also know a lot about the day-to-day things that can tip people who are vulnerable to depression into a low mood. And they're all those annoying things that we all should be doing regularly — eating well, getting enough sleep, making time for socialising and connecting with people, and not overindulging in alcohol, drugs or high fat/high-sugar foods.

And of course, exercise. But you'd be forgiven, especially if you spend too much time on Instagram, for thinking that exercise is a silver bullet. There's certainly no shortage of people claiming to have cured themselves of depression by exercising, and of course urging others to do the same. Don't get me wrong, there is some truth to it — in the most general sense exercising more is never a bad idea. However, it isn't a silver bullet even if it's worked for you.

At a behavioural level depression is marked by inactivity — whether that be mental or physical. It tends to make us want to crawl to the back of the cave, pull the duvet over our head and avoid what feels hard. If you've found yourself feeling low and emotionally flat after being laid up with a virus for a few days, that's the behaviour of inactivity creating the feelings of depression, because that is how we work — our behaviour can also create feelings. Think of jumping around and getting yourself amped up for a sports game, for example. We act excited and fired up to create that feeling.

In this way, increasing activity of any kind can help shift our mood, and exercising regularly can certainly help to ward off depression. But the main problem with most exercise advice is that it is a particular kind of invalidation — the oversimplification invalidation. To say to someone who is struggling with depression that they need to exercise more is tantamount to saying they need to just get over it and feel better. Because getting active when you're in the grip of a period of low mood is asking too much — it's asking you to do the hardest thing that is most hard.

The more helpful version is to focus on activity — not exercise. This includes mental activity and engagement with mental tasks. The point is to get moving in whatever way feels achievable. For someone who is starting from a baseline level of doing a reasonable level of exercise, this may very well be exercising more, but for someone who is housebound and struggling to get off the couch, it might simply be getting up and walking to the letter box or around the block. In short: it's important to set yourself up for success and start from where you are. Once you are moving and feeling like your mood has lifted and the depression has passed, that's the time to set up some easy-to-maintain activity goals. Because being active is a great way to keep depression at bay. What is referred to in medical terms as relapse prevention.

Much the same thing can be said about mindfulness, another oft-touted silver bullet for all our modern ills. I'll cover mindfulness more in the following chapter but suffice it to say that sitting quietly and paying more attention to our internal experience when we're depressed is not very helpful, in fact it can be dangerous. Why? Depression already forces us inwards. It tends to make us ruminate or over-focus on negative thoughts and painful things in a loop — that for those experiencing it, it can feel inescapable. Asking someone to focus on their thoughts and let them come and go, if they are afflicted with ruminative thinking, is like asking someone to run before they can walk — it's too much.

So again, caution and some minor alterations are required. If you do find that getting stuck inside your negative thinking is an issue for you, then externally focussed mindfulness might be worth trying. Rather than focussing on our thoughts, find things outside ourselves to focus on. Nature can be good, focusing on what is passing us by as we walk, drive, or commute. Focussing with intention on podcasts, music or other auditory stimuli. In this way, we can still practice one of the core skills of mindfulness — deliberately moving our attention and focus onto things we want to pay attention to — without risking increasing ruminative thinking. And much like exercise it is also an excellent relapse prevention approach — the research supporting traditional mindfulness shows it's effective at reducing relapses when people practice it when they are *not* in the grips of a depressive episode.

Who wouldn't be depressed?

I believe it's impossible to be truly objective, about anything really, but specifically, about the cultural times we live in. It's like the air we breathe, it just is. And separating ourselves from it is only possible in retrospect and even then, it's not entirely objective. But to return to the beginning of this chapter, who wouldn't be depressed? At the time of writing this, we are tentatively easing our way out of the largest pandemic in a hundred years, facing down wildfires, floods, heatwaves and other extreme climate events seemingly one after another. Unprecedented has become a tired descriptor, at least in part because it's no longer true. This is, to utilise another tired phrase, our new normal.

As people have tried to understand the increasing levels of depression and anxiety over the last few decades, at least in the West, it's hard not to look outwards. To capitalism, inequality and the growing impacts of climate change. On inequality we have pretty clear data, that in short suggests the higher the levels of inequality within a society, the worse off — on average — everyone is.

It's too easy to see inequality as just impacting those on the lowest rungs of the social ladder, but it doesn't. I mean of course the impacts of poverty are real, and you are better off if you have more. But compare any decile of an unequal society with the corresponding decile of a more equal one, and the more equal is better off across the board on a whole range of avoidable health impacts, including mental health and addictions. Everybody is relatively emotionally healthier in more equal societies, whether poor or rich.

Of course, this research can be used for all sorts of political arguments. But to me, the main point is regardless where you fall on the political spectrum, there is something about how we've organised modern society that is making us more miserable, even for those we might deem successful or wealthy.

We're very used to thinking about the impact of pollution or carbon-creating activities. We're even trying to come up with ways to mitigate the impacts of escalating carbon dioxide and other greenhouse gases in our planet's atmosphere. Economists classify much of the pollutants of the twentieth century "externalities".

The concept of externalities refers to situations where the effect of producing or consuming various goods and services creates costs (or benefits) on others that are not reflected in the prices charged for the goods and services being provided. Carbon credits and offsets are an attempt to cost these externalities so they can be accounted for, and through the economics of cost and pricing, reduced.

Perhaps we should be thinking about depression, anxiety and other escalating and avoidable mental health struggles as externalities of capitalism and inequality.

And if that is true, and I believe it is, then the very least we can do is make sure that we keep pushing to ensure that treatment, support, and help are available and accessible for all who need it. Even better to reduce the structures that cause the problem in the first place.

In the meantime, you as an individual can't of course change society. But you can at least work to redress some of the imbalance in your own life. If you have enough, help others out in whatever ways you can. Don't let your work consume you, and if your work requires more of you than you can give, work towards a role, a job, or a career that doesn't. And generate gratitude, don't fall into the trap of trying to keep up with the Jones's, because it's increasingly clear that the Jones's, despite their new car and flash house, are likely to be struggling as well.

We can't do it on our own

Perhaps the most damaging impact of depression, especially ongoing chronic depression, is that it takes us away from people. For many people, isolation is the outcome, as they pull away from those who are close, driven by a deep sense of something being wrong with them. So awfully distorted does this thinking become that I learnt in the early days of my career to not ask parents who were depressed, suicidal and desperate to think of their children because when someone is in this space, they genuinely believe that their loved ones, even their children, would be better off without them. So dark has their self-relationship become that they feel themselves to be toxic, perhaps even damaging to be too close to. Depression becomes the assassin of love.

Like love, the words to adequately describe the experience of depression seem inadequate. It's hard to convey the despair and the certainty with which the feelings warp reality to suit their dark and hateful view of oneself. The brutal truth is that sometimes the suffering of depression can also become a self-fulfiling prophecy. Sometimes people do give up on those with intractable depression, it can be too hard to be around, to keep trying to care for someone that is so unmoved by the attempts to reassure them or to make them better.

But we don't need to make them feel better. Hope doesn't come from being cajoled out of despair or convinced one is wrong about the feelings they have. Sometimes all we can do is be there, and while that's hard — at least emotionally — it's also easy to let go of having to help, fix, or change things.

And if you are in the grips of despair, your task is also hard, but simple to do. You have to let them be there. You don't have to believe you're loveable to make use of the love of your family, or your children or your therapist.

You just must believe they're crazy enough to love a clearly unlovable person such as yourself. You can't do it on your own, and hopefully, you don't have to. Because hope is just a belief, an idea. Hope is imagining a future that is positive. It doesn't have to be true — because true or false doesn't apply. And while it is possible to start building hope on one's own — to help oneself — love and hope are so inextricably entwined that I'm not sure it's possible to have one without the other. Not because it makes the future happily ever after, but that it keeps making the tough times worth it.

SUMMARY
- On average, depressed people see the world more accurately, which is to say to be optimistic and happy we have to learn to filter the world in a particular way. It's important, therefore, to look for what works, not what is true, when it comes to figuring out how to see ourselves and the world.
- Common psychological "tricks" like improving our self-esteem or positive affirmations, generally don't work because they try to convince us of something that doesn't feel true. Better instead to focus on self-compassion and changing how we feel through enacting different behaviours. Simply put, feeling pride requires us to do things we feel proud of.
- Seemingly self-destructive behaviours, like addictions for instance, make more sense when we see them as attempts by people in pain to feel better, even if only briefly. Addiction can happen when the need to not feel pain is high, and the relief from drug use provides a high level of relief.
- Rising levels of inequality worldwide, and in Aotearoa, are one of the key factors to the rising level of mental distress. Inequality harms all of us, even those who have the most, by turning us against each other and the required competition for resources.
- Depression isolates people, and this might be the most harmful impact of all. Helping someone who is depressed can be as simple as being there, and being present. If you struggle with depression the most important challenge is likely to be to let people who care about you act as if you matter. Because you do even if you don't feel like it.

CHAPTER 5:
Mindfulness and the benefits of quieting the mind

THERE'S AN EXPERIMENT I OFTEN QUOTE, published in 2014 that makes the — literally — shocking claim that people would rather subject themselves to a painful electric shock than sit quietly in a room on their own with nothing to do.

In the experiment, people were asked to sit in a room, empty apart from a chair, with nothing to do — no devices, no distraction — for fifteen minutes. They did have access to a button, which they were aware would deliver a painful but harmless electric shock via a strap on their ankle.

Do you think you could sit for fifteen minutes with nothing but your own thoughts? Or would you be tempted to shock yourself?

In this experiment, at least a quarter of women chose to shock themselves, and two-thirds of men did. People would rather cause themselves pain than sit quietly with their thoughts.

Now, like any study, the results have been questioned and of course there may be other motivations for choosing the shock option, and without doubt, the gender difference is interesting. But fundamentally the fact that anyone would struggle so much to just sit quietly for only 15 minutes is worthy of our attention.

It's likely you've heard of mindfulness — often touted as a cure-all for our modern psychological ills. The rise of mindfulness makes sense to me as it actually responds to a very important — and some would say growing — problem. Namely, our collective fascination with distraction, as evidenced by our compulsive use of our mobile devices.

So, what is mindfulness?

Secular Buddhism

I'm not a Buddhist, but it's not an exaggeration that they were the first research psychologists. Putting aside any conversation or critique of their theology, of which I have only the most passing basic knowledge, the overlap with Buddhist approaches to mind, emotional equanimity and compassion have rightfully bled into Western psychological thinking from as early as Jung and his wider spiritual views on our emotional wellbeing.

More recently, people like Jon Kabat-Zinn with his Mindfulness-Based Stress Reduction (MBSR) which is an approach utilising Buddhist meditation techniques to better manage chronic pain and other health conditions, along with Marsha Linehan's Dialectical Behaviour Therapy (DBT) have bought mindfulness meditation to the Western masses.

And now apps on your phone will promise to help you meditate your way to better sleep and better wellbeing.

I came to mindfulness meditation — with its roots in Zen, Vipassana and Tibetan approaches to meditative practice — through my involvement with a DBT treatment programme for Borderline Personality Disorders. As mindfulness was a core part of the treatment, we enlisted a lovely man who was a Buddhist monk to conduct a weekly hour-long meditation class with our clients. Tenzing was his adopted name, and I greatly enjoyed attending his sessions myself for a number of years.

For something that sounds so simple, it's not easy. I often explain it as being like exercise, especially weight training. The point is not getting strong, it's staying strong. You never get to a point where you can bank the gains and stop, having completed the task. You have to keep up the practice to keep fit.

Like training at the gym, it makes you stronger in your general life. The gains you see across the week are your ability to focus, catch runaway thoughts and moods quicker, and for many, a clear reduction in anxiety.

In theory, it's as simple as sitting still, and focussing on an anchor, most often the sensations of the breath, and dispassionately observing what your mind does. What actually happens when you do this is you realise what a tangled mess your mind is most of the time, and you get drawn into thinking the thoughts, or thinking about the thoughts. Some thoughts are stickier than others, some effortlessly float by. Emotions, especially worry and anger, are particularly sticky.

And the practice is to keep bringing the spotlight that is our conscious attention, back to the breath and away from getting dragged around by the reactiveness of our mind and its thoughts.

Let me tell you it's not always easy, and it can be a little confronting to feel so inept at something seemingly so simple. However, non-judgementally there is no "good at it", only noticing. Observing what our mind does, and in that way getting to know ourselves — and our internal world — better.

Without a doubt it is a skill we can all get better at, just like fitness. It is also a skill that has its roots in 1000's of years of practice and thinking — and not just in Buddhism. In reality, all religious traditions have some form of meditative practice even if they don't call it that.

Mindfulness has become so relevant and seen as a needed panacea in many ways because we train ourselves out of it through the normal habits of everyday life. I'm no anti-technologist. I love my smart phone, and the ease of online life, but we are increasingly drawn by addictive algorithms to not pay attention to the present. Instead we glue our eyeballs to a plethora of entertainment options literally at our fingertips.

Avoidance of emotional states has always been a "thing", and a necessary and healthy thing. Being able to take our attention off our emotions when they're troubling us and focus on things that either make us forget our worries or even better, shift our feelings, is a relief and a necessary skill for life. However, too much distraction leaves us feeling out of touch, disconnected from ourselves, listless and missing the very important messages our emotions are trying to signal to us.

Ultimately, it's a balance, between experiencing internal emotion-focussed attention and avoidance (outward distraction-focussed attention). Too much in either direction can be unhelpful. And while we've always had distractions in the form of short-term fixes — alcohol, drugs, anonymous sex — distracting ourselves has never been easier. And as a direct result, mindfulness, or at least learning to be quiet and pay attention, has never been more necessary.

Blind to what's there

Of course, given that mindfulness is at least thousands of years old, its appeal is not just about modern ills and our technology-driven distraction. It actually taps into and makes us aware of some fairly basic mechanics of how our minds work. In fact, how consciousness itself works.

We are all observers of our consciousness, in one way or another. And we generally take it for granted that other people see, hear, smell and experience reality more or less the same way as us. But what we take for granted as what we "see" is not "real" at all.

This is the sort of thing cognitive psychologists, along with philosophers, spend their careers studying. How do we know what we know, what is consciousness and how do we perceive the world?

To take one basic example. Our eyes, much like an old pinhole camera, actually "sees" the world upside down, in that the image that makes it through our retina, and lands on the back of the eyeball is in fact upside down. We also have a small blind spot in the middle of our field of vision, where the optical nerve connects to the back of our eyeball. What we see is a constructed image, with instantaneous image correction, using information from both eyes, and assembling a vision in the back of our brain.

Perhaps not such a basic example after all: vision, across all species really is mind-bogglingly amazing. So, are we seeing "reality"? Well, a lot of species will see something different depending on the wavelengths of light they perceive and whether they have binocular vision, as just two examples.

Your dog sees a different world from you. Which is real?

This is true for all our senses, and how our attention generally works. Think about the last time you were in a room with a ticking clock. You likely heard it, you may have even gotten frustrated that you couldn't stop hearing it, but it's also likely the once you were engaged with something else you stopped consciously hearing it.

Our attention simply filters it out. Our brains do this all the time. It's not an exaggeration to say that our minds are lazy and get lazier as we get older. Or perhaps "more efficient" might be a better way of saying it. We are pattern-recognition machines, and the more experience of life and our environment we have, the less work our brain has to do to perceive the environment. It takes in the barest amount of information and fills in the blanks based on experience — quite literally in the case of our vision.

We start life as prototype pattern-learning machines, as massively flexible organisms, taking in, adapting to, and learning from the environment we find ourselves in. Our flexibility as a species in this sense is our biggest strength. We are biologically identical to human beings that lived in the most basic of material circumstances thousands of years ago, yet here we are biologically the same in a vastly more complex world, learning and adapting, generation after generation.

It's fascinating to me that as we age, we actually end up with fewer neurons as we learn. As patterns are established, neurons die off. We set up networks in the brain and discard those we don't need. It seems counter-intuitive — you would think as we learn more, we need more space for learning and memory, but that is to see the brain like a modern computer with ever-growing hard drives.

Our hard drives actually get more efficient over time, but as a result, they can also get more rigid. To recognise patterns, and respond efficiently, based on prior knowledge and experience, is normal — but also has its limitations. The observable, everyday example of this is how we all have a tendency to get set in our ways, less flexible, and more prone to habit, as we age. It might be relative to how open-minded and flexible to change we were to start with, but generally the trend is the same for all of us. The flip side is experience and wisdom, work getting easier, being able to make accurate predictions and knowing how to successfully handle a wide range of situations.

It has served our species well.

Returning to mindfulness, one of the deeper learnings from meditation, is to start to observe these mental patterns. And as a result, increase our capacity to see what is actually there, not what our pattern-recognition machines think is there. To work on seeing as much of reality as we can. Quite literally, to expand our minds.

Psychedelic renaissance

Expanding your mind was pretty big in the sixties when LSD was everywhere and people were "turning on, tuning in and dropping out". And after 40-odd years of being illegal and banned from almost all research, science has turned its attention once more to the impact of psychedelic drugs such as LSD ("acid") and Psilocybin ("magic mushrooms"), as well as MDMA ("ecstasy").

As treatments, administered in carefully monitored environments, they show a lot of therapeutic promise. As they also did before being made illegal by worried conservative governments around the world, threatened by a counterculture of young people unwilling to blindly follow the status quo. Because what psychedelics do is widen our perception and shake up the rigid patterns of how we perceive the world.

Now, this is not a "pro-drugs" pitch, but I am very interested in how these drugs can help people where other treatments may fail. Let's just look at it in simple terms, what they do to our brain. To see someone on LSD is to see someone perceiving reality differently. They seem alert, stimulated and as if their brain would likely be more active than normal. It would make sense to assume the drug itself would be stimulating the brain.

In fact, it's not quite that straightforward. Studies into the mechanisms of LSD show that one of its impacts is to dampen the regulating part of the brain called the Default Mode Network or DMN. This part of the brain is like an organising centre, a traffic controller that restricts and controls how different parts of the brain communicate with each other. It's central to the sense of "self" and central to experiences like daydreaming, self-reflection and thinking about our past and future.

When we're meditating, we see changes in the DMN. In the brains of experienced meditators, the DMN is less active — as it is when someone has taken LSD.

The experience of deep meditation and psychedelic drugs is not that dissimilar, but of course LSD is quicker and stronger in its effect. User reports from clinical studies are clear, that a therapeutic psychedelic experience allows people to think more openly, to abandon unhelpful habits or patterns (like smoking and addictions for instance) and to see the world more clearly. *The Doors of Perception* are opened, as the autobiography of Aldous Huxley described in his experience of mescaline — another psychedelic compound.

You don't need to take a trip to alter your habits and patterns, it's likely conscious attention, medication and, of course, therapy will be sufficient. But as we've been discussing up until now, being such effective pattern learners is a real problem if the early patterns you adapt, learn and habituate to are unhelpful, lacking or otherwise abusive and damaging. If we rigidly hold to our ways of being, for fear of strong emotions, anxiety and change. Of course, those patterns, feelings and ideas are experienced as "who we are" — they feel like they are "us".

And this is where things get a bit, well spiritual. With high doses of LSD and other psychedelics, users experience a loss of self — an abandoning of "ego" or, as some call it, an ego death. People in the grips of highly religious experiences talk about similar experiences, as do experienced deep meditators. As an experience, it is very hard to put into words and describe, but to have the experience is deeply powerful and for many, transformative. At a brain level, as the DMN is less active and behaves in different ways, our sense of self can change and be more fluid. Rigidly held ideas about ourselves, about life-events and relationships can be experienced differently.

This sort of experience is as old as we are as a species, and modern research has shown it is a highly effective balm for those who are struggling with death anxiety in response to terminal diagnoses. It is also beginning to show effectiveness for depression and PTSD.

There is a lesson for all of us in this, one that doesn't necessarily require us all to drop out. It's that when we hold tight, too tight, to our ideas of ourselves — we can cause ourselves distress. Rigidity is the issue, and it is human nature. It's understandable, but it's also a good idea to make sure you're incorporating things into your life that encourage and indeed require ongoing flexibility and challenge.

That might mean making sure you're always learning and trying new things. It might mean not getting set in your ways. But it also means spending time around children (who are naturally mentally flexible) and people who don't see the world the same way as you. If you have the resources, it also means travel, exposing yourself to new places, cultures and new ways of doing things.

It may also mean meditation, which might be as simple as spending distraction-free time in nature.

This is because one of the drug-free ways to open our minds is to experience "awe".

Awe is the feeling you get when you're in the presence of something vast that challenges your view of the world, and your place in it — most often in nature. Awe, like psychedelic and spiritual experiences, challenges us to see that our ego or our self is a construct. When we see beyond it, to the ways that we are actually all connected, it leads not only to positive feelings but also to an overall sense of wellness.

We stop being so attached to "me" and feel more like "we". Self-help, becomes instead, "all help".

There's a reason why it is the core of the most successful (in terms of membership) peer support programme in history — Alcoholics Anonymous. The central role of "God" in AA can put many people off before they even get through the door to their first meeting. But interestingly enough, Bill W., one of the co-founders of AA, actually credited his own psychedelic drug experience on Belladonna (another plant-based psychedelic compound) with helping him find sobriety, and this was reflected in his focus on the spiritual in recovery — as well as his early advocacy for LSD as a treatment for alcoholism.

For some, AA may lead to organised religion, but when you look at how they actually talk about God, there's a lot of focus on letting go and accepting one's powerlessness, of not letting our over-inflated sense of ego get in the way. Of surrendering to a power greater than oneself.

That's awe and dissolving the ego as much as anything else.

This is one of the beautiful paradoxes of spending a career exploring consciousness — which is another way of thinking about what therapy is, what the psychedelic writers call being a "psychonaut". Yes, part of the answer is to find ways to get more comfortable with yourself, to be better company for yourself, and to make the internal voices more gentle, more loving and more forgiving.

But it's also helpful for there to be less self. To dissolve the ego more frequently and feel a sense of connection to the wider universe. And at the risk of sounding like an old hippie, to be more at one with everything, not just yourself.

SUMMARY

- Increasingly, modern life seems to make it harder to simply allow ourselves to be with our thoughts and be comfortable with our own company.
- Devices, distractions and endless busy-ness can drive us into avoidance as a lifestyle, and in doing so decrease our ability to tolerate our internal experience.
- Mindfulness is not a panacea but a range of flexible approaches to what life throws at us. It is a useful counterpoint to the rigid avoidance of ourselves, in that it provides a way to practice being "with" our internal experiences in a non-judgemental manner.
- Humans are habitual pattern-learning machines, and our learned, rigid expectations can blind us to reality and what is really there, making change hard — and closing our minds.
- Meditation and more recently psychedelic therapy have both shown that increasing our mental flexibility and making our minds more able to adapt and change can increase our emotional wellbeing. There is also some evidence this is how common anti-depressants work.

CHAPTER 6:
How to calm our emotions

THERE'S ALWAYS A RISK with oversimplifying, but I've become increasingly convinced over the years that all of what ails people who seek out therapy can be traced back to one root cause that I've talked about a fair bit so far: emotional dysregulation. Sounds like a good piece of psychobabble, but let's dive into it a bit more.

Recall the last time you were really distressed, overwhelmed or upset. There was no doubt a reason, and you also likely moved out of that state of high emotion after a period of time. Maybe as part of that experience, there was some time where you felt like your emotions were out of control. That out-of-control feeling is what we call "dysregulated" or not regulated. The feeling of coming down from the distress and back to relative calm is what we call regulating our emotions. And a state of relative calm is returning to balance.

Think of your emotional system as a hi-fi stereo, with a big powerful amp and an old-school analogue volume knob that you turn clockwise to increase the volume, and anti-clockwise to decrease the volume. Most of the time our emotions rumble along in the background like pleasant background music that we can hear and tune out if we're having a conversation or working on a task. But when we get upset the volume increases and demands our attention. If we attend to our feelings, and have good emotion-regulation skills, we can gradually turn the volume back down to a pleasing level again. Feeling emotions doesn't mean being dysregulated.

But perhaps we struggle to regulate our emotions. So, when we get upset the volume stays up, or only turns down a little bit. Then the next thing that crosses our path and causes distress turns the volume up again, and before we know it, we can't hear ourselves think — the music's too loud — and then we start to get distracted and upset about how intense our emotions are. It might then only take a relatively small trigger to tip into overwhelm, or what some people call distress.

At this point, to continue the metaphor, the speakers are distorting and it's impossible to even hear the music clearly anymore. Now imagine that the volume knob is also stuck at full volume and can't be turned down. This is a state of emotional dysregulation.

This "straw that breaks the camel's back" problem is key to understanding the complexities of invalidation. Because most of the time when we get told we're overreacting, freaking out, or otherwise "feeling too much", we aren't feeling the wrong thing, we're feeling too much of it.

The problem isn't the music, it's the volume. Because it isn't possible to "feel the wrong thing" — but it is entirely possible to have a faulty volume knob that makes it hard to get the volume right and control the intensity of the emotions we feel day-to-day. At first glance, how does this "explain everything"? Surely, not all emotional challenges are about high emotions or distress? They're not, but if we expand on this a bit then it becomes clear.

All mental health struggles can be seen as a direct experience of dysregulated emotion. It is a form of numbing or blocking out the distress, or as behaviours developed in response to trying to manage dysregulated emotions. We can think of the behaviours we use to respond as being either flexible or rigid responses. But more about that later.

And to expand — or possibly stretch to breaking point — our metaphor, then sometimes we turn the power to the whole house off at the mains to get the stereo volume down. Or we do all sorts of possibly harmful things to try and block out the noise of distorting speakers — hide under the bed, cover the speakers with duvets, block our ears or attack the speakers.

When we can't regulate ourselves, it can feel like we are going crazy. Our emotions feel like they're of no value, broken and like they offer no helpful information. And it can be very hard to manage these states on our own.

Relationships and co-regulation

Sometimes we all need a hug. No matter how old we are, a hug, a comforting hand on the shoulder or even just a pat on the back, helps. Not surprisingly science agrees. Another one of those oft-cited studies, which has been replicated many times, shows that merely holding our intimate partner's hand can increase our tolerance for pain and cause a number of our physical markers to synchronise with them. This has been dubbed "interpersonal synchronisation". Brain waves, heart rate and even breathing can synchronise as part of this phenomena. To any couple who has been through childbirth, this will make absolute sense to you.

Even more amazingly, a follow-up study seems to suggest that our intimate partner just being in the same room as us, with no physical contact and without speaking at all, can also have a positive impact on our pain tolerance, and that the higher the levels of empathy, the bigger the effect. While studies haven't been done on various other kinds of relationships, such as a parent with a sick child, close friends, or even just genuine caring professionals, like nurses or palliative care workers, I would bet that we would likely see the same impact. And it's also likely that the effect would be related to how close we feel the person is to us. But feeling what the other person feels is the mechanism. Empathy regulates people.

Again, we can't do this stuff on our own as well as we can with others. Even when we build up our resilience to pain and suffering, we're generally drawing on a close relationship and the experiences of that, to help us manage those times.

Occasionally, I'll have clients say to me some version of, "I don't know what you're doing, but it seems to be working," as we find ourselves a few sessions in and therapy is starting to make an impact. And we know from research that the biggest factor in successful therapy is the relationship, the sense that you click with the person you're talking to. And the, "I don't know what you're doing but ..." is the presence of a highly empathetic human while we experience emotional states. And at the risk of blowing my own trumpet, I believe high empathy and the ability to sustain high empathy with a range of people is the core skill of any competent psychotherapist — or pretty much any helping professional for that matter.

We can sometimes get so lost in trying to find, or define, the latest therapeutic trick, or the latest model of therapy that is being touted as the new empirically proven approach. But it can be hard to accept that much of what helps people is the simple fact that we need others to help us learn about and tolerate pain. We have covered how that works (or doesn't) in childhood, and we'll talk soon about how vital and challenging love is as adults, sometimes as a consequence of our childhood. But in many ways therapy is a uniquely constructed version of this very human phenomenon. And while sometimes being able to just sit quietly with someone in distress is surprisingly powerful, as we start to use words to describe what we're feeling the process gets supercharged.

Finding the right words

Apparently, there are around 3,000 English words that describe emotional states. Even then, there are still words in other languages that describe subtle emotional distinctions that we don't have a word for, the German word schadenfreude probably being the best-known example. It means, incidentally, the pleasure we derive from someone else's pain or misfortune.

Language has developed and enabled us to communicate a wide range of subtle emotional states we experience.

And the words we use about feelings matter because they help us to regulate. Just describing an emotion with words can helps us reduce its intensity. Emotional literacy is a vital emotion-regulation skill.

It also seems to matter that we say it either out loud or via writing. Saying it in our head is important but describing how we feel is even more regulating when we express it to others. Even more so if we express it in the context of an empathic relationship.

I think of the various words we have for feelings as like one of those big fold-out paint charts, which have the little squares of different paint colours. There will, for instance, be a whole page of greens, all sorts of different shades, and yet all undeniably green. Emotions fall into large groups, what we call primary emotions, and while like anything there are a number of varying theories, there is a general consensus that there are six primary emotions.

Fear, anger, joy and sadness are the easy ones. Then it gets tricky, but we include love, which some people prefer to describe more broadly as interest, guilt and shame (which are different but often get lumped together) and disgust. Surprise is, surprisingly, important too in that it is core to how we navigate the world. So, we end up with a list something like:

- Fear
- Anger
- Joy
- Sadness
- Love
- Guilt and Shame
- Surprise
- Disgust

Fear

Having already covered fear in the section on trauma, let's just say we have a lot of words for it because there are lots of versions of it. From the mildest nervousness, a tickle of trepidation through to full-blown horror. It exists for obvious reasons: to keep us safe from threats, and to motivate us at a biological level, as adrenaline and our nervous system to fire up and prepare for harm. Generally speaking, it makes us want to run away. If it flips into angry fear, it can make us fight.

Anger

We all know anger, from its subtle version, irritation, to the more complicated jealousy — anger plus love and possessiveness — through to blinding rage. Necessary for survival, it's the "fight" in the flight-or-flight response and it makes us lean into situations. Whether it be a threat that we attack or an obstacle that we need to overcome. Road rage highlights that it can be helpful (by motivating us to get through the traffic jam) but can also be unhelpful in its negative versions.

Joy

Buddhists have a view that joy can only be found in the moment. The mindfulness literature talks about "cracking open the moment" to find joy. Through our basic reward structures joy makes us want to repeat behaviours that promote it, and this is where we find happiness, contentment, elation, ecstasy and pleasure. Whilst it's easy to think of all joyous feelings as positive, repeating words that make us feel good isn't always good for us though (see page 74 on Affirmations).

Sadness

The natural response to the pain of loss, adjustment or changes is most painful when it's about the loss of relationships that are central to our lives — attachment relationships. Grief is the obvious example, but also loneliness, missing someone, or just feeling a little glum. It tends to motivate us to withdraw and focus on the loss, to enable us to — ideally — adjust, heal and move on.

Love

While I've covered romantic love, and attachment as love, this emotion gets much wider if we think of it as interest, attraction, longing and desire (both sexual and non-sexual), affection, kindness, caring and compassion. More than just motivating us towards that which we are attracted to, it also promotes engagement and interest and leads to commitment and prolonged attention. We can experience all these feelings for people of course, but also things, objects, places and even just ideas. Obsession, patriotism, or dogmatic beliefs are examples of the less positive versions of love and interest.

Shame/Guilt

Ultimately, shame is a social emotion, as it signals to us we have contravened a social rule and done something that others will disapprove of. Embarrassment is the milder version and guilt is the more rule-focussed version when someone has done something "bad" as opposed to disapproved of. Vital for collaboration and communities, it can be easy to get over-focussed on crime and the ways people don't respect the law, but society is actually held together by the fact that most people rightfully avoid shame and guilt by largely doing the right thing and following the rules.

Surprise

Shock, surprise and amazement all serve to stop us in our tracks and cause us to pay attention to something that is happening that is out of the ordinary or contrary to expectations. It serves an incredibly necessary function by motivating us to pay careful attention to figure out if what we have observed is a threat. Getting a fright is the everyday version, but it also includes awe, a feeling that is uniquely positive and promotes very intense attention.

Disgust

Physical disgust has its emotional correlate and causes pretty much the same behaviour — wanting to get rid of, expel, or get away from the subject of the disgust. Largely we can think of it as many different forms of not liking. It serves to protect us by causing us to stay away from things may harm or even poison us — literally, or metaphorically by transgressing our values or ideals. Being disgusted by someone or something can become physical — even causing us digestive distress, "They make me sick ...."

And just like paint, we can mix these various emotions in all sorts of weird and wonderful ways. Fear and anger for instance give us emotions like hatred; joy and fear yields excitement; disgust and joy can result in tantalising intrigue or perverse pleasure.

Of course, while we can measure the emotions listed above, largely because they are clearly defined, universal across all cultures, and have biological correlates, generally speaking, we're not all walking around hooked up to biological sensors. So, we rely on self-observation and learnt experience to differentiate and identify what we're feeling.

What is a feeling?

All emotions are physiological reactions to some form of stimuli, what is called an "affect.". Our nervous system identifies this reaction, and after registering an affective experience our brain and consciousness respond by motivating behaviours. We can also consciously observe the state, label it with words, and then choose to act — or not act. Of course, some reactions are much quicker to motivate behaviour than others. We may react to someone sneaking up on us instantaneously without apparent conscious thought, or we may mull over the feeling of lustful attraction to someone for some time before deciding to ask them out on a date.

As a rough guide, each of those steps — stimuli or trigger, affect, communication to the brain, action, conscious thought and decision to act or not, can form a focus when we are trying to work on emotions that are tricky for us. For example, let's consider what is commonly called "anger management".

In general, we want to increase our capacity to observe and understand all facets of an emotion to bring it under more conscious control, starting with getting familiar with what sorts of things make us angry. It might be due to external triggers, like being told what to do by someone we don't respect, being cut-off in traffic, or mulling on past frustrations in our minds. A trigger will then lead to a physical response, generally an increase in heart rate and blood pressure, a tendency to over-focus on the source of frustration by decreasing peripheral vision, and then a desire to do something.

All this needs to be identified and noticed by the brain, and the first thing we might experience is the desire to act — to lash out, yell, swear or otherwise fight. We can then use words to identify, regulate and make conscious efforts to not act, or make choices to reduce the levels of emotional stimulation.

If, as we've talked about previously, we haven't had a lot of validation, or even acknowledgement of our emotions, then we might not be very good at identifying the signs, even at the earliest stages of just noting and interpreting physiological responses. This can be the impact of invalidation, and neglect in particular — the pathways that lead to noticing are not strong. This is also one of the ways that the deliberate practice at just noticing, or mindfulness, can be useful in increasing our ability to self-observe.

If we notice, but cannot label our feelings, then it can become harder to slow down and make different conscious choices, and harder to communicate what's going on. We also miss out on the natural validating impacts of language. And, if we struggle with all these stages, then we run the risk of a dysregulated emotion hijacking our system, bypassing our impulse control and decision-making, and we act on anger. The red mist descends, and we lash out with aggression.

Dysregulated emotions can lead to out-of-control behaviour.

Of course, in reality, we can all be hijacked by strong emotion, but it's also true we all have different thresholds, and different levels of ability to do each of these steps. Not enough sleep, consuming alcohol, or even just having had an emotionally filled day can also shift these thresholds.

In terms of managing, in this case anger, we can also intervene at each of these steps. We can work on creating a generally more balanced state, through healthy choices, exercise and practising relaxation exercises. We can better monitor what goes on from the neck down, we can work on slowing down our general level of reactivity through mindfulness and tolerating — without acting — a wider range of emotions. And we can get better at identifying, labelling and perhaps most importantly talking about, our frustrations.

All of this requires practice — no matter how good you may feel you are at it.

Distress and overwhelm

This system — physical sensations; experiencing; identifying with words; and choosing to act or not — fails all the time, for almost all of us. And even if it doesn't lead to problematic observable behaviour, we can still get very lost in the experience of feelings we can't identify. It can feel like we are going crazy when we're in the grip of strong feelings and don't know what they are or why they've arrived. Nonetheless, it can still be helpful to acknowledge this for what it is: overwhelm or distress, or as some prefer "tension". Either way, just being able to describe the subjective experience in words is a start. It helps get our thinking mind back inline because we need that to be able to label an emotion. To find the right words we need to be able to place what we're experiencing in context, and to understand how we are personally seeing it — what spin we're putting on the events that lead to us feeling that way. We all have these filters, things that bother us or cause us to feel certain ways, that are individual and different to how others might react in the same situation. Generally speaking, we call this ability to understand and reflect on what we're feeling insight, and it's a skill that's easier when our feelings aren't overwhelming us.

Of course, this is a catch-22 situation. With dysregulated emotion, when we are overwhelmed, we can't keep our thinking inline, and to be able to self-validate we need to be able to keep our thinking in line.

This is where we need other people to regulate us. Just as a mother calms a distressed infant, or the mere presence of a loving partner can ease the suffering of their spouse, we need another mind to help us regulate ourselves. And it doesn't have to be anything magical or even particularly active, just the presence of an empathic person we trust can be enough. Sometimes just the calming voice of someone we have never met on the other end of the phone can be enough.

Just rack it up as one more thing we can't do on our own.

The problem of stress

It's always amazing to me how easy it is these days to wear your stress and "busy-ness" like a badge of honour. How frequently is the query "how are you?" met with, "really busy!"

One of my all-time favourite book titles is *Why Zebras Don't Get Ulcers*. It is title of a great guide to stress by Robert Sapolsky and my favourite book on the subject.

It has many useful things to say, but its central idea is that stress, as a problem, is unique to humans because our ability to think and plan is our biggest strength, but also our worst enemy. In much the same way that anxiety relies on our imagination to conjure up a fearful future event, stress relies on our planning and ability to anticipate and plan tasks.

What we've talked about as the fight-or-flight response is common to most animals, including zebras and humans, and operates as an alarm and resource allocation system. Most of the time our fight-or-flight mode is turned off, but when a threat is detected we switch into readiness mode and physically prepare for action.

This is all perfectly normal, and necessary. The ability to detect and run away from a lion, if you're a zebra, is vital. As is the ability to calm down and focus on eating grass once the lion has gone away.

The problem is, as humans, we can spend too much time in this fight-or-flight mode, and when we do so it can create physical and mental harm. Not being able to switch off our survival mode burns us out.

I've never been chased by a lion. In fact, it is very rare for my life to be threatened in any way. But our brains, and our ability to plan and think about the future, can make everyday things feel life-threatening. Getting that report in on time, getting that promotion, and making the big sale can all feel like life-or-death even though we know rationally it isn't.

This is the key difference between what we might describe as anxiety, distress and stress. Stress relies on a very clear and definable external trigger — anxiety relies on imagination. This is not the same as saying stress is real, and anxiety isn't, but we can usually identify something very concrete that is causing our stress.

The challenge to modern-day stress then is to both get better at "turning off" our fight-or-flight response and examining more thoughtfully what our beliefs tell us are life-or-death problems.

Waiting for motivation

Motivation may be one of the most written about self-help topics, which tells us it is something that is key to the human condition, and something we all struggle with at times. It can also be — in its absence — a key indicator of depression.

It's common to think about motivation as something you either have or you don't, and if you don't, the answer is finding some. The question is where one might find it, and how to go about the search? Well for many, including those who are experiencing depression, that can become the Holy Grail.

Simply put, motivation is a desire to move or get active, to act towards a desired goal. Its opposite, apathy, is the absence of the desire to act: even if we can think of what we desire — we simply can't get moving.

Many (many) years ago I played first-fifteen rugby with a young man who liked to prepare for the game by punching, and at times head-butting, concrete block walls in the changing room. Now as ill-advised as this was, it was also highly effective at creating motivation. The pain caused him to feel anger and aggression. It was very motivating for him, albeit a little scary for the rest of us. It certainly made him play better.

Now, before everyone gets outraged at me for condoning self-harm, the point is this: we can wait for motivation to arise naturally, which is wonderful when it does, and is what many of us think of when we talk about "feeling motivated". Or we can create motivation through behaviour that is designed to bring about the desired state.

The problem with depression is that the behaviours of depression, namely being inactive, and having an inward focus, is in itself demotivating. Excessive and repetitive thinking is a feedback loop that creates and maintains a demotivated state.

Ultimately, it's one of the very practical ways that medication helps. Anti-depressants don't "fix the brain" so much as it enables behaviour that breaks that downward, de-motivating behaviour loop. The same goes for exercise: activity is the behavioural opposite of depression's unrelenting lethargy.

If you're searching for motivation, there's no need to bang your head against a wall, you need look no further than making small, maintainable behavioural changes. Any activity is better than none, any movement better than lethargy, any outward focus better than rumination. The trick is to not let your low mood convince you that small efforts are pointless or pathetic. Anything helps, in that it enables the next step and the next ...

So stop waiting for motivation, create it. While that might feel like hard work, I think the idea we can ultimately treat ourselves with deliberate changes in behaviour is liberating. It gets easier once we get moving and literally take the first step. It can also help — or even be vital — to have someone helping us along the way and taking those first steps with us.

Just don't wait until you feel like it.

Too sensitive

When we talk about the different ways we can learn regulation skills, and over time get better at reducing our levels of emotional distress (learning how to calm down), some people feel that they are just "too sensitive".

When people ask me if maybe they're too sensitive, I always challenge them: "According to whom?" because, as the saying goes, it takes two to tango. It can be used as a get-out-of-jail-free card for the unempathetic in our world. In the worst cases, it can be a way for bullies to turn the tables and victim blame.

There are indeed individual differences in how emotionally sensitive to the world and relationships we are. As I've outlined previously, temperament plays a role. Some of us are just born more tuned into our emotions.

It's also undoubtedly true some people could also do with being more sensitive.

What makes emotional sensitivity a problem though is how it's responded to. For people who do feel things more, it can be harder to learn to tolerate strong emotions, and any problems, like trauma for instance, tend to be amplified.

This can set up a feedback loop where an individual gets emotional, is invalidated for this (you're just "too sensitive"), which leads to the individual getting even more upset. Over time, this makes things worse because our emotions *are* us. Our responses, our views, and our reactions to people define how we think about ourselves. And if we come to believe that our emotions are wrong, it's just a hop, skip and jump to believing something is wrong with us. This is one of the impacts dysregulated emotions can have on our identity and how we think about ourselves as a person.

Research into the soothing power of our intimate partner tells us how effective their very presence is, and how this is directly related to how empathic they are. To flip that round the other way, it also makes sense that if the person reacting to us is *not* empathic to our current plight, then at the very least it won't help. At worst, as many of us have experienced, it will amplify the distress.

Passionate, caring, creative, and empathic are all positive ways of thinking about strongly emotional people, but when the world keeps telling you, "You're too sensitive" it can be hard to hold onto the positives.

However, while feeling things strongly can be uncomfortable, and for some people can cause problems, the solution never lies in getting rid of our responses or becoming less sensitive. The solution lies in better understanding what we feel, and why, and finding ways to validate and honour ourselves through thought, words and deeds.

That doesn't make us feel less. But it will make us feel better. And through regulating ourselves, and allowing us to help, will give us more balance.

Resilience

If there's one buzzword in mental health I hate, it's resilience.

It's easy to sell. Who wouldn't want to be more resilient? More able to cope with life's up and downs, better able to manage stress, less susceptible to negative emotions, and more able to quickly bounce back from adversity.

There's no doubt resilience is "real". Evidence shows when you look at groups of children, and adults, exposed to similar sorts of pressures, stresses and traumas, some do less-worse than others. These individual differences in broad terms are understood as being caused by differences in resilience.

So, what's the problem? If we can teach these skills, why shouldn't we?

The problem ultimately is not with resilience, it's with the way it is increasingly touted as a modern-day panacea and a cure-all. Even as a solution to problems that are way beyond an individual's control.

Resilience, by definition, focusses on individuals, and in practice has become the twisted new version of "personal responsibility". Mental wellbeing as defined by capitalism.

Resilience training — in the absence of meaningful policies to address inequality, poverty, homelessness, addiction, sexual and domestic violence, and a swathe of other community problems that assail our lives — is just the new "harden up".

Looking at resilience retrospectively makes sense —

what makes some people cope better than others is a valid area of study.

But as government policy, it borders on irresponsible. If you literally have the power to influence the circumstances that cause suffering, why wouldn't you? Why choose to spend time and money on just helping people cope better with adversity when you could instead choose to reduce their challenges?

Teaching resilience without addressing the massive social problems we're increasingly facing is like teaching people to swim in response to rising sea levels.

Because even the best swimmers get tired, and without higher ground to swim to we all drown. If we are to look at resilience, then in my view we should be looking at what makes for resilient communities, resilient families and resilient systems of support. Because otherwise, by telling people, and especially young people, that they simply need to be more resilient without acknowledging or addressing anything else that may be going on around them in their lives or their communities, we may as well be telling them to just get over it.

Breathe

There's a very good reason why, when we learn how to meditate, we're asked to pay attention to our breath. It's always there. It's also one of the most obvious aspects of what is called homeostatic regulation.

Homeostasis is the natural processes that maintain our bodies' natural state of equilibrium via things like breathing, heart rate, temperature regulation, blood-sugar levels and other largely invisible processes that happen regardless of whether we're aware of them. For instance, as we are now familiar, with our fight-or-flight response, when we move into that state of readiness due to anxiety, all sorts of physical processes move into action. Our heart rate increases, our pupils dilate, blood drains away from our extremities and our digestion shuts down. Our body prepares for action.

Most of this feels like it just happens, and indeed homeostasis is outside consciousness most of the time. We can observe it, but not necessarily control it. Or can we?

There are well-validated examples of long-term meditators — Tibetan monks mostly — who have spent their whole lives practising meditation, and as part of this training are able to bring various unconscious bodily functions under conscious control. One example is the ability to raise the temperature of their extremities, so they can tolerate sitting in the snow without getting cold or frost bite. In a similar way free divers, who dive without tanks and hold their breath for long periods, practice bringing their suffocation reflex under control. Most of us can only hold our breath for about 30 seconds, but with training that can be increased to two to three minutes, with some free divers being able to do around 10 minutes!

Now you don't have to be a free diver or join a Buddhist Monastery to get some control over your physiology. You just need to pay more attention to your breath. It's the easiest and most obvious of our physiological reactions to control, and the one that can actually make a huge difference with practice. Most of us will have been told at some point — or have told ourselves — to take a deep breath, and that can be useful. But what is more useful is to get better at seeing our breath as a useful piece of data to understand our likely responses, or how stressed we might be. Think of it as an early warning system.

And the great thing is, you don't need expensive equipment, apps or courses, just a clear commitment to pay attention. One of the easiest things to do is to make sure you breathe deeply enough and to practice doing so. That's as easy as placing your hand on your diaphragm, just below the ribcage in the centre of your abdomen, and making sure that when you breathe your hand moves. Deliberate deeper breathing can shift our state from fight-or-flight to a more balanced state. Most relaxation exercises you'll read about, or will be encouraged to practice, are an example of this in one way or another. Of course, the opposite — shallow breathing — where we breathe with just the upper part of our chest, without moving our belly, can bring about anxiety.

The key here is practice, as it is for almost everything we've talked about in this chapter. Calming down is entirely possible when we get more familiar with what not being calm looks and feels like. The more we learn to not be afraid of what we feel, the more familiar we can get with our own reactions and reflexes. And in doing so, we can work to make choices — to respond not react.

SUMMARY

- Emotion regulation is the ability to manage and control our emotional responses. It is not the same as being calm, it is being able to manage our emotions and not let them get the better of us. For instance, you can be extremely upset, and still regulate your emotions.

- We need others to help us regulate. We learn to regulate our emotions early in life through relationships with our caregivers, and we need connections with people to help us regulate ourselves throughout our life.

- Words and language are a key part of regulating our emotional responses. Just speaking words out loud to describe what we are feeling is in itself regulating and validating.

- We can regulate and validate our emotions through action, as well as using deliberate action to increase the emotions we want more of by acting "as if" we feel the way we want to feel.

- Regulating and managing our physical body is a highly effective way to regulate emotions. The most well-known example of this is altering and managing our breathing. Learning breathing exercises is a vital emotion-regulation technique.

CHAPTER 7:

How to care (but still look after yourself)

OCCASIONALLY I HAVE CLIENTS STOP mid-sentence, look at me with a slightly concerned manner and ask, "How do you listen to this all day?" It's a fair question, and one I always try to answer honestly.

Burnout, or more specifically "compassion fatigue" is a real professional concern, sort of like the "RSI" of the caring professions. Psychotherapists, in particular, are required to undergo their own therapy as part of training, and all talk therapy professionals are also required to attend "supervision". Supervision is essentially a session of their own once a week or fortnight, with a senior colleague to discuss and support their work.

But what happens when we care too much?

Caring is a scarce resource and it's not just professionals who can burn out. Many people find themselves, in their relationships, friendships, dealing with with elderly parents, or in the workplace, feeling that their "well of compassion" has run dry.

At the more extreme end, vicarious traumatisation is a recognised response to working with traumatised people. It occurs when the mere experience of talking with highly distressed, traumatised people can leave the recipient experiencing symptoms of trauma themselves.

Empathy makes the experience contagious.

Compassion fatigue is less obvious, and is at least as much about a lack of care for yourself, as too much caring for others. Symptoms of compassion fatigue can include feeling mentally, physically and emotionally exhausted; feeling cynical about work or a caring relationship; and feeling disconnected from emotions.

Ultimately, relationships operate on give and take, and if a relationship is a one-way street this is not the natural state of things. So whether you have a job in the caring profession, or circumstances mean you find yourself caring for an ill or incapacitated family member — it's vital to keep trying to re-balance the scales.

Personally, I've never been much of a fan of bubble baths and scented candles, but I appreciate that everyone has different ways of caring for themselves. Therapists call it self-care, another great example of giving the obvious a label.

Ultimately, it's about being helpfully selfish, but that idea can be a hard sell to people naturally inclined to care for others. And even though it's a tired cliché it's true you have to put your own oxygen mask on before you help others.

The thing about being selfish, so you can help others, is only *you* know what you need to refill your tank. And only you can give yourself permission to do it.

Because truly caring means being selfless AND selfish. You can't have one without the other.

Putting yourself last

Of course, some people would say it's possible to care *too* much. We even have a way of describing it — being a "people pleaser". But who wouldn't want to please people, and how could that be a bad thing?

What we normally mean when we talk about being a "people pleaser" is someone who tends to put others' needs, wants and desires ahead of their own. And there's the rub.

Balancing needs in relationships — our own with those of the other person — is a constant juggling act. Sometimes we give, and sometimes we receive. The ebb and flow is normal, but if all the giving heads in one direction then it tends to create problems.

Resentment is the biggest red flag. If we are unable to say no, to set limits, or stop ourselves from being generous, resentment is inevitable. But it's also a trap of our own making when we're the one offering too much, not communicating, and not tending to our own needs.

Why do people allow themselves to give too much? Generally, it's because we feel like our worth is defined by what we give: to be loved, valued and cared for we must put the other person first.

Upbringing plays a part: being overly valued for what we do, rather than who we are; expressions of our needs or wants being invalidated or made to feel wrong; a parent who needs looking after in some way — alcoholism is a common factor. All these things require the child to abandon themselves and focus on the parent being "OK".

Traditional gender roles also play a part. The role of "wife" or "mother" can lend itself to giving with little expectation of return. But it's not the giving that is ultimately the problem.

It's the absence of healthy selfishness.

Being selfish is usually considered an insult, but normal selfishness is a useful and challenging way of thinking about how to listen to our own needs more. Most people feel guilty when they behave selfishly, but if you're prone to people pleasing, you're likely to feel guilty any time you put yourself first.

And of course, the mechanics of healthy selfishness often come down to one important word:

"No".

How to say NO

Such a little word. Just two letters, but not being able to say it can be downright dangerous and can also quickly make life unmanageable. Even if you're safety isn't at risk, too many "yes when you mean no" moments lead to resentment: the wish to be agreeable eclipsed by exhaustion, and the growing pain of our own needs and wishes being ignored.

The real problem though is when our belief in our value is so skewed towards what we do rather than who we are, then the possibility of disappointing others takes on an extra dimension: What if they don't like me anymore?

Childhood, schooling, our work-obsessed culture, can all convince us that our value, our sense of self, lies in what we do. To be useful is to be valuable. The problem with this is it means our self-esteem, our regard for ourselves, is conditional.

Conditional on what we can achieve, and what we can do for others. Learning to say no is not just about practicing the use of the word, although that can be useful: one strategy is to practice saying no to things that don't really matter.

But ultimately what helps is to work on changing the way we value ourselves. To make our belief in our self-worth unconditional.

This is one of the cornerstones of what is known as self-compassion. The idea is that our worth is not measured through achievement or action, but is inherent: all human beings are deserving of love and have value.

Even you.

Saying "no" then becomes an act of self-care. A way of being able to actively value ourselves, to put ourselves first, and consider ourselves worthy of care and attention.

Such a little word, but so important.

All of this might sound rather fanciful, but if you're someone who habitually says "yes" to everything, and regrets it, you'll know what I mean.

However hard it is to do, it's important. But just coming right out and saying "No" can be a bridge too far. So, a useful strategy can be to just slow things down. Say, "yes, but I need to think about it," or "I'm not sure, I'll get back to you."

Give yourself time to think and see it as an opportunity to value yourself. Because when we say no to others, we are also saying yes to ourselves.

Sometimes though, helping others can not only be at your personal expense but even futile.

How to validate

If you're going to do one thing when someone is depressed, anxious or feeling any painful emotion it is to "validate". It's not only helpful when people are struggling; it's pretty much the single most effective relationship strategy.

So while I've talked about the impact that invalidation can cause, what is validation, and how do you do it?

Validating is more than just listening, it's giving the other person the experience that we understand and accept how they're feeling, and why they feel that way. It's not telling people what to do or how to think or feel differently. When we do that, we "invalidate", sending people the message that what they are feeling or thinking is wrong, bad or too much.

The thing with being validating is we don't even have to agree with what they're feeling, or believe that we would feel the same way. We just need to show we understand that given everything we know about them, we get that is how they're feeling.

That might sound easy, but actually, it takes practice. Most people trip up on the acceptance bit. Acceptance is not the same thing as agreeing and a lot of people find it hard not to try and calm the other person down, or the even subtler version, convince them "everything will be fine". This is well-intentioned but invalidating. Otherwise known as the "calm down" problem.

But far and away the thing that makes validating hard is that for one reason or another we're often too busy thinking about what we're going to say next, rather than listening. And often, because emotions are hard, we are wanting it all to go away. We don't want to feel those feelings ourselves.

So the real key to being able to validate people, whether they are depressed, angry or just upset, is to slow down, take a breath, tolerate our own feelings and responses, suspend judgment and work to fully accept and understand (not necessarily approve of) the other's point of view.

When we manage to do this, real empathy happens. Not sympathy or understanding, but actually letting the other person know we get what they feel. It's what therapists mean when they talk about feeling "connected" and it feels good to be on the receiving end of it. It also feels good to be on the giving end.

Talking about your own experiences, giving advice, and helping the person see a different perspective, these can help sometimes, but not if you start there. Generally, it's a better idea to start with validation and save those other things for later. And sometimes, just feeling like you are understood, truly deeply understood, is enough on its own.

Like many things, empathy is a skill and requires practice. But what to practice, and how to practice are tricky questions and require an understanding of how empathy works.

People commonly confuse empathy with sympathy, but they are different. When we sympathise, we feel warmth or sadness about the other person's situation or emotional states. Empathy, by contrast, is the experience of actually *feeling* what the other person is feeling and communicating that to them through words or deeds.

Interestingly, it seems there is even a particular kind of brain cell or "neuron" dedicated to helping us feel what others feel. Human beings (and some higher apes) can learn from observing others, and when we observe others, our brain responds like we are actually doing the activity ourselves. One of the parts of the brain that is active when we're observing and rehearsing actions in our mind is called "mirror neurons" and they're an important part of how we empathise as well.

Which leads us to the first, and most important tip when it comes to being more empathic: we have to increase our level of comfort with emotions in general. Because empathising involves tuning into the emotions of others, we have to be open to actually feeling them, and individually we all have varying levels of comfort with emotions.

How do you do that? Practice. By increasing our own capacity to feel our own emotions, we are also practising our ability to be open to others. It's a win-win.

The horse-to-water problem

You know the old saying, "You can lead a horse to water, but you can't make it drink"?

There can be lots of reasons why individuals don't want help, but let's focus on denial, which basically is a means of organising our experience in a way that minimises pain (If it isn't happening, it doesn't hurt.)

We can all likely think of times when in hindsight we were "in denial" about the reality of a situation, and normally because we didn't want the truth to be true.

Whether it is our health, our weight, a relationship breakdown, alcohol and drug use or just the fact we are unhappy about where we find ourselves in life: denial is something we can all recognise because it's such a fundamentally human experience. Although, by its very nature we don't usually recognise it until later.

So how can you help someone you care about who may be in a state of denial about their own emotional health, or even more of a challenge, their addictive behaviour?

Well, put aside any ideas you may have about challenging, or confronting them, or Hollywood-style "interventions". They very rarely work. And when you think objectively about why, it's obvious: it creates resistance and reduces the chances people will be open to thinking about their own behaviour.

So while you can lead a horse to water, if you force it to drink you risk drowning it.

In general, we need to approach gently and help the person reach their own conclusions. "Motivational Interviewing", a particular counselling approach used with people in denial about their addictions, suggests starting with information to just get the person thinking about their own behaviour. But don't rush to "action", because if the person isn't ready to make changes, this will also turn them off.

And as difficult as it can be to accept, we may not know what will help them. While it may seem obvious to us, unless we really understand the problem the other person is having, we can't be helpful.

But we can talk with authority about what the consequences are, and the impact on us. The classic example is if we're concerned about someone's drinking. It isn't likely to be helpful to point out, "you drink too much" but it can be helpful to talk about the negative consequences. And as I've already talked about, it's absolutely important to understand that the person is likely struggling with things that you may or may not know about — they're doing the best they can with what they have.

Which, of course, isn't a reason to accept abuse, bad behaviour or attacks. But neither should we think that getting tougher with someone who is struggling is the right response. Boundaries, distance, and keeping yourself safe are all personally good approaches, but the idea of "tough love" — usually employed by desperate families to try to help out-of-control loved ones — is not something I've ever advocated. Trying to use the connection of a relationship to get someone to act the way you want them to is not only unhelpful, it may even be abusive. Cutting off, reducing or managing contact with someone is a different thing, but it's important we own doing these things, and in doing so do them for the right reasons.

Control and Boundaries

Saying no, or more seriously, cutting someone off because of abuse or hurt are examples of what we call "personal boundaries," another piece of popularised psychobabble that has made its way, usefully, into everyday language. But it's worth taking a moment to clearly define what they are, and how to work on them.

Boundaries are an individualised relational map, that we all have, that allows us to maintain our sense of self, and our individuality, by being clear about what is "me" and what is "you". Boundaries define psychological, emotional, ideological and behavioural (real-world) space.

Our sense of where our boundaries are is defined by what we say yes to, and what we say no to; what we allow, and what we forbid; what we crave and what we detest; who we love and who we dislike; whether we hug our friends or prefer a firm handshake.

And when you really start to consider it, we have multiple boundaries, and they vary from relationship to relationship, to place and setting. As therapists love to say, "it depends". We have our professional friends, our close friends, our family and our partner. Where they sit within the map of overlapping and at times tangled up imaginary fences is complicated in theory, but we all know exactly where they are as soon as somebody bumps up against them, or barges right through them.

Whether it's a workmate asking about our sex life, a friend of a friend turning up on our doorstep at 1.00 am, a cousin asking to borrow money, or a parent wanting to hang out with us and our friends when we're teenagers, when they've been crossed we know it. And some of the above might not even seem like a transgression to you, because they're all examples I conjured up of my own boundaries. Yours are likely to be different.

Reflecting on how you define and manage your own boundaries in relationships can be an extremely useful starting point for understanding the problems we all run up against in relationships.

Problems with saying no, needing to be liked, or struggling with others' disapproval and causing upset, is a problem of boundaries being both too permeable (not saying no) and too far flung (taking responsibility for things that aren't "ours") — other people's emotional responses, for instance.

Being unable to let other people get close, or struggling to be intimate, open up, love and form close relationships is an obvious example of boundaries being too rigid or self-protective. But then again so is not taking responsibility for our very real impact on others. Whether it is the hurt we cause or just not thinking of others in a way that furthers relationships — calling and checking in, remembering other's birthdays, or details of their life. We tend to refer to people like this as self-centred.

Violence and sexual assault are always boundary transgressions, by definition. They are examples of acting as if there are no boundaries, at least for the victim, or worse, that ignoring them is part of what the perpetrator values in some perverted fashion.

Control is the belief we are responsible for, or have a say over, things that aren't actually within our control. It can be thought of as a boundary clash or overlap, when someone feels that parts of what we might consider "ours" falls within their boundaries — at least according to them.

In some relationships, this is of course, fine. Parenting involves having responsibility over a lot of day-to-day decisions of our children's existence. Gradually easing these boundaries over time is healthy parenting. We also take legally approved power over the rights of our aging parents or others too infirm to manage their day-to-day affairs. It's little wonder that these situations of sanctioned and necessary power over others can easily slide into abuse. The conditions rely on power over being used for the benefit of the other, and healthy boundaries of the one with the power. Exercising this power well is a pretty good definition of love, but more on that later.

In short, people whom we might view as controlling are struggling with boundary confusion. Ultimately this kind of boundary confusion is an attempt, albeit a harmful one, to manage difficult emotions.

The "calm down" problem is the thin end of this wedge. When we are invalidating people in this way, we're trying to get them to stop feeling and expressing emotions that cause us to feel things we can't tolerate, as I've laid out earlier in this chapter. More intense versions of control, especially in intimate relationships can of course be dangerous, so I want to be clear that working to understand this kind of controlling behaviour doesn't equal approval. While pushing back clearly and assertively is required when control shows up, it needs to be acknowledged that in intimate relationships safety should always be the first consideration — and if safety is at threat, then please, seek support.

However, in friendships, professional relationships, or an intimate relationship where you are safe, if you're feeling controlled then it can help to see it as firstly solely their problem, and secondly as a boundary clarification issue. Saying no, being clear about what we do and don't want, and not allowing another person to dictate our reality can be hard work because it can literally feel like we're pushing their boundary back away from us while reasserting ours. But it's necessary work. This brings us to how to give feedback, and having difficult, caring conversations.

Striking when the iron is cold

No one likes being told what to do, and fair enough. We tend to like it even less when someone's pointing out something that feels like "constructive" feedback. Nonetheless, receiving feedback from others is vital to our growth, and learning to give it is vital for our wellbeing. In most relationships, we all have a tendency to strike while the iron is hot, to say whatever it is that is bothering us at that moment. As a result, we say it when we're most likely to be in the grip of strong emotions or dysregulated.

Having strong emotions coming at us from someone who appears to be upset with us is likely to make most of us resistant, and as a result less likely to be open. Arguments themselves rarely lead to helpful change, for this very reason. When we're both dysregulated and rigidly resistant, learning can't happen.

So the old guide from non-violent communication traditions is to instead strike when the iron is cold — to give the feedback, to say what we need to say, when we're both calm, and more likely to be open and receptive. Of course, it can be hard, because at these times, when things are going well, it can be too easy to talk ourselves out of saying something that might lead to upset. But it's much more likely to work.

Two more principles are useful: our old friend "I statement", and avoiding judgements when describing observable behaviour.

"I statements" are one of those clichés most people are familiar with, and for good reason. Starting a statement with 'I' makes it much more likely to be an effective form of communication. But a better way to define it is to only talk about things within your own boundaries, and the impact on you of the other person's behaviour. Starting a statement with "I" doesn't magically make it less attacking — you can still say, "I hate the way you ..." which is the sort of thing we're all prone to say when the iron is hot.

However, when we focus on talking about our own feelings, and any descriptions of behaviour being as non-judgemental as possible, then we increase our chances of getting our message across. Therapists talk about a therapeutic window, where optimal conversations take place. Too dysregulated, and we can't hear or take in new information. Not interesting enough, and we become bored, unfocussed and unable to stay connected. This window might look different for each of us, but generally, if someone's not getting upset, and you feel like you have their attention, then you're in the window.

Of course, if you're prepared to give, then you also must be prepared to receive. And again, this comes down to being able to stay regulated and think about what the other person is saying, even if it's challenging. Having said this, no one should put up with bad behaviour, and if what we get back is attacking or abusive then putting down the blacksmith's hammer and walking away from the anvil altogether is always a good option.

The last principle is time and patience. Most of us need a bit of time to digest and think over feedback we receive. That's OK, and even though our urgency to say what we think can make us impatient, it's important to allow the other person space and time. What they do with what we've said isn't up to us, it's outside our boundaries.

And we're all getting this wrong, all the time. "The Serenity Prayer", the cornerstone of Alcoholics Anonymous (AA) Twelve-step Programme says it very succinctly:

"God, grant me the serenity to accept the things I cannot change, the courage to change the things I can, and the wisdom to know the difference."

Knowing the difference, knowing where those boundaries lie, that's a lifelong lesson.

When we get it both wrong and right

Emotions can be like viruses. We can catch them from each other, and some of us are more likely to catch them than others. Some of us are just more sensitive to tuning into the emotions of others. We think of people like that as empathic or sensitive — but it can be a burden, especially if you're not aware of it happening.

Think of a time where in talking with, or being around someone, a feeling has really gotten under your skin. You may be still feeling it sometime later. It's like you've caught the feeling, and struggle to get it out of your system. This often happens with anxiety in social situations. Maybe you're aware of feeling really anxious in response to interacting with someone at a social event, despite having no conscious reason to feel that way.

Maybe it's me? You think to yourself. Maybe you even convince yourself that it is. If you do, you are likely thinking unflattering thoughts about yourself. You've made what you're feeling fit an internal narrative about yourself.

"I was feeling anxious, because I'm useless in those environments, I should never have gone. They clearly didn't like me, they could barely make eye contact, and left the conversation as soon as I took a breath ..."

And later you realise that it was actually the other person who was anxious, and you picked up on that feeling. And — like we all have a tendency to do — you made it about you.

You felt the right feeling, but you misinterpreted it — you were both wrong and right.

This can happen in close relationships all the time, where we feel we've done something wrong because the other person is in a bad mood and we decide they're angry with us, and before we know it, we're having an argument and it's come true.

I also believe it's behind a lot of problems we experience in work politics, where people who spend a lot of time around each other pick up on the feelings that inevitably swirl around us as we go about our daily business in close proximity to each other. In our own unique, dare I say neurotic way, we make those feelings about us — "I'm sure she doesn't like me" — and a narrative grows around our mistaken perception.

It can be easy to fall into black and white thinking about this, to decide we have to either be right or wrong — she either is or isn't upset with me. That's normal with emotions, it's what strong emotions do. What's harder is to stay curious and open to the idea that maybe it doesn't have anything to do with you.

Already you can see there are a couple of ways that we

can take a wrong turn in this process. First, we can feel something and decide it's "ours" not realising we've picked up on a feeling that isn't our own. And secondly, we can accurately detect that someone else is feeling something but get the "why" wrong.

In both instances our empathy is accurate, but our interpretation of it is wrong.

This dynamic is one of the key reasons people who train to become psychotherapists must have therapy as part of their training. Think of it as learning to use your empathy correctly. To be able to accurately discern what are our feelings, and what are somebody else's.

The first misread — wrongly picking up something as our emotion — is a boundary issue. Through therapy, we learn to get better at discerning what is ours and what isn't, and we get more familiar with how we tend to react in different situations. The second misread — getting the reason behind the emotion wrong — can be more complicated. Generally, when this happens it's hooking into some aspect of our own story. It could be a subtle trigger for past experiences, or ideas we hold about ourselves. For example, if we pick up someone is annoyed, and have had past experiences of people being annoyed with us but rather than talking about it directly, they reject or punish us, it is easy to slide into anxiety and fear that the person is going to leave or otherwise abandon us. We can even know that this is what is happening — we can have quite clear insight into this process — and at the same time, it still happens.

Like any repeated past experience, getting familiar with the trigger helps. It also helps (even though it may feel hard in the moment) to ask directly, "You seem off, are you OK? . . . Can I just check, are you annoyed at me for some reason?"

The reason why this can be hard is the understandable fear that they will say "Yes, I am"! But it is also hard because when we are in the grip of strong emotions, it can be hard to move towards what we fear. But like all fears, the only way to unlearn a misread fear is to keep moving towards it, so we learn a new ending to the old stories.

SUMMARY
- Caring for others is seen as a virtue and caring too much for yourself is seen as selfish. However, in reality it's about balance. When we care too much for others, we can burn ourselves out, or stick to rigid rules about how things should be in relationships.
- Saying "no" is a common issue for people in therapy, and ultimately being able to say no is about boundaries — being clear about what is your stuff, and what is other people's.
- The single most powerful relationship strategy is to understand, practice and get good at being "validating" — of both others and ourselves. It is a flexible approach that requires us to accept differences and understand that accepting another's point of view is not the same thing as agreeing with it.
- We can only help those who want help. Therapy is a treatment of the willing. However, people not changing in the way we want, or when we want, is about us, not them. It's possible to both support people and be patient about change.
- Managing conflict in relationships is about timing. Knowing when to talk about something, rather than just following our feelings, is vital. "Strike when the iron is cold" is a useful guide.

CHAPTER 8:
Exploring love — and hate

ROMANTIC LOVE MUST BE the most commercialised emotion in all of history. Fear, based on the trillions of dollars the insurance industry has made, maybe a close-run second. But throughout human history love — and desire — have formed the centrepiece of the overwhelming majority of art, writing, music and culture. As a species, we're obsessed with it.

I'm sure when the first hominids picked up a rudimentary brush and began painting on cave walls, some of what they were expressing was the ecstasy of love or the pain of rejection.

This duality — of ecstasy and pain — is why love is such fodder for creatives. It is the fuel behind some the most beautiful works of art, and some of the worst atrocities, in history. In our modern-day life, our intimate relationships are, for most of us, the source of our deepest satisfaction, but can also be the most dangerous. Intimate partner violence is the most likely form of violence that women will experience, and the psychological impact of relationships — good, bad, traumatic and otherwise — is the reason many people end up in therapy.

What is love?

At the risk of being thoroughly unromantic, it's important to define in broad terms what love is, and how it works. Romantic love is deeply hard coded into our being as it can result in offspring. The urge to reproduce is the most basic evolutionary need there is. But like most things to do with human beings, it's a lot more complicated than that.

There are many different models of love, but the simplest is often the best. I believe love can best be understood as happening in three phases:

1. Lust
2. Falling in love
3. Commitment/Attachment

These aren't necessarily clear and distinct phases, and we can cycle back through them over time, but it is a useful map.

Lust, of course, is the exciting bit. The chemistry of instant attraction, longing, the feeling of being drawn to someone for reasons that sometimes even we can't explain. It's the most obvious example of how powerful our unconscious mind is, as most of us have a "type" of person we are attracted to. We may not even be aware of this until we start to notice patterns in our adolescence and early adulthood. Lust or mutual chemistry is, of course, not the same as any objective or cultural definition of attractiveness. Beauty really is in the eye of the beholder.

While it's easy to jump to the conclusion that lust equals sex, I think it's broader than that — but it often is physical. The first touch, the first meal, the first kiss. It operates as a kind of magnetism that draws us together and the novelty of newness holds us together until we figure out if there is more there. This phase can last for a while, but it's often short, maybe even only one night. But it's certainly measured in weeks at most, not months.

The falling in-love phase is a period of rose-tinted glasses, where the connection grows beyond mere lust and the other person becomes part of our internal world. We see this in one of the tell-tale signs of falling for someone: when we cannot stop thinking about them. In therapeutic terms, we've internalised them.

It's quite a wondrous obsession, though not without its potential dark side as we will see, but in its healthy form is quite wonderful. This is the phase of poetry, of flowers, of seeing the wonderful in everything — and especially the object of our affection. It is the foundation of attachment and the beginning of a bond that glues us together and at a biological level, allowing for our genetic survival via offspring. Children need the protection of adults and a mother needs the support of their partner most acutely in the early days of child-rearing. I don't mean this in a narrow, morally conservative way, but human beings mostly pair bond, and largely mate for life, or have a series of mates throughout their life. Of course, there are exceptions to this — culture is a powerful factor — but most people will settle into at least one close relationship at a time. This phase is measured more in months than weeks, but not years.

Over time, falling in love settles into attachment, mature love and commitment. Hopefully, by this point, we've gained a more realistic, grounded view of our partner — while still remaining their biggest fan. At this point the "glue" of attachment has set, we have shaped our psychological reality to the other person, and likely our practical reality as well. This phase can, at least in theory, last forever. It's also true that for most people this is when the problems of love show up. The excitement of lust and the adoration of falling in love can mask issues, or mean we miss them entirely. Our early attachment experiences can either set us up for success or future problems, but one way or another our past does come back to haunt us.

Despite everything I've said, love cannot be objectively defined. Of course, we all share similarities in our relationships, many of which might be culturally defined. But love is not a greeting card, a rom-com or a happily-ever-after. At times it's incredibly hard work.

Love is defined for each of us by our past experiences, through our earliest attachments with our parents. From behaviours we experienced as their love for us, as well as what we see, hear and feel about the relationship between the adults in the house.

These experiences create a map — a set of expectations — for how we should be loved, what kind of love we deserve and how a relationship should operate.

It's important to be very clear at this point because we are about to enter dangerous territory. Understanding the ways in which our past can impact the present when it comes to relationships can easily slide into victim blaming, and it can also easily be misunderstood as victim blaming.

This is the limitation of a one-way conversation, via the written word, as opposed to a two-way conversation, where you, dear reader, are instead sitting in front of me, and we find our way through this material together. Nothing I'm about to say in the rest of this chapter should be taken as apportioning blame for bad behaviour to the person being impacted by it. Violence is wrong and should be admonished. We know that most of the impact of interpersonal violence is directed at women by men.

It's also possible to be unhelpfully simplistic about the impact of childhood. Not everyone who grows up in a violent or abusive home will end up in a violent relationship as an adult — either as victim or perpetrator. But, as I've already outlined, we are all unavoidably shaped by our development.

However, as with all feelings in relationships: they're

bigger. We get more dysregulated by what happens in our intimate relationships even if we're pretty much able to regulate ourselves everywhere else in our life. In fact, I'd say that difficulties in a relationship would be the most common non- "mental health diagnosable" reason people attend therapy. The obvious reasons to get upset in a relationship, are, well, obvious. Affairs, unsustainable conflict, different values around parenting, religion, sex or money. These things aside, relationships are largely a collection of small things, and each is an opportunity to regulate or dysregulate each other.

Emotion-Focussed Therapy or "EFT" is a particular therapy that focusses on the impact of attachment styles and development to untangle the conflict and emotional tangles couples get themselves into. But most relationship therapy focusses on this very simple, yet hard-to-put-into-practice idea: how do we respond to each other's emotions, thoughts and ideas in ways that work? In ways that are on average, good enough?

It can be helpful to think of a relationship as a literal container, a large wooden bowl for instance. A bowl can only hold so much water before it overflows — in the same way a relationship can only contain so much emotion before things become uncontained. Bowls can also leak if they have cracks in them, where in this metaphor the cracks might be trauma, abuse and past, damaging experiences that mean the needed relationship skills are not present. We can also break the bowl if our present-day actions are egregious enough, such as violence or betrayals.

For example, we may have a couple that largely gets along well, and both have had a relatively stable upbringing. However, they hit a whole lot of difficulties in their life all at once, say having young children, work pressures, redundancy, health issues, or the loss of a parent. At that point conflict and distance may show up, because the bowl isn't able to contain what for them is a novel amount of distress. In this situation the task is to expand the bowl — to mutually build the capacity to tolerate more emotion, both in themselves and others.

On the other hand, we may have a couple who have both experienced past trauma. When conflict arises, one or the other is triggered into safety behaviours — avoidance, withdrawing, switching off, or aggressive responses — and the relationship suffers damage. There are cracks in the bowl that need to be mended for the relationship to be able to contain what it needs to.

At the risk of over-extending the metaphor, the Japanese tradition of "Kintsugi" is a wonderful way to envision this. This is the practice of mending broken pottery with gold as the glue, highlighting and accepting the imperfection as something that is then part of the history of the object — not something to try and hide. In this tradition, the repaired vessel becomes more beautiful, and more valued.

A relationship that has been through things together, needed some help, and survived is without doubt stronger. As I write this, I've been with the same person for 23 years. We're not married, but we do have children together, which to me is even more of a commitment than marriage. But whatever your commitment is, it only matters that there is one because the glue of attachment is meant to hold us together through tough times. To give us time to repair, or grow, the container. The intimacy and depth of love and respect gained over time can't be bought or replicated. That's the true gold.

Reigniting the spark

So, you're committed, you've grown and repaired the bowl. Why, to some, does it end up feeling like you're living with a flatmate, not a lover?

It's not unusual for people in a long-term relationship to struggle with emotional distance and feel that as a result their connection has faded or been lost. It's a natural and common mistake to feel that the absence of that feeling means something. It does — just not what you think it does.

It's also a very modern problem. When both partners need to work full time to make ends meet, balancing childcare and perhaps caring for elderly parents, their relationship can very easily fall off the priority list. At the same time our conception of modern love often tells us that one person has to be our everything: our soul mate — love never-ending.

From a behavioural point of view, over time we fall out of the habit of doing loving, connected behaviours. Like many busy people in this increasingly hectic world, we can prioritise the "busy-ness" of being married over loving behaviours. Everything gets done, and at the end of the day, we land on the couch with the TV on, both parties on their phones, distracted, out of touch and not talking.

Now, this might seem like a long-winded way of saying "book in a date night" — and in some ways it is. Taking the time, if resources allow, to do something special like going out to dinner is always a good idea.

But more important than pinning it all on big-ticket items are the small, everyday actions that demonstrate a loving relationship.

It might be helpful to think back to what you did regularly when you were in the honeymoon period. Did you hold hands in public, hug more, kiss when you left the house in the morning, have sex more, sit closer together on the couch?

The three phases of love: lust, falling in love and

commitment aren't linear. One way of thinking about them is places you've been to, that you can always revisit. If you're feeling bored, flat or otherwise not attracted to your partner, talk together about how to revisit or revitalise lust. A "naughty" weekend away is the clichéd version. Or if you're feeling unloved, unappreciated or that the emotional relationship has cooled, think about how to refocus on falling in love. For instance, celebrating anniversaries, reengaging with what you fell in love with about the other person, or even renewing vows.

Whatever you do though, make sure you break it down into small enough behaviours so that you can do something every day. And if you don't already, build in just ten uninterrupted minutes to talk to each other every day. No phones, no distractions. Ask how their day was, and then actually listen. This was easy when we were falling in love, when we wanted to spend all our time with the other person and were naturally fascinated with everything that came out of their mouth.

Ultimately, long-term love isn't the big things. It's a collection of small things, practised regularly.

The problems of mismatches

So far, I've made tackling problems, and making a long-term relationship last, sound easy. It's not of course. It's simple, but not easy. And it's even harder if there are some areas where we feel like we have a mismatch with our partner. One of the common examples of this is where one partner is experienced as, or described as, "needy" by the other.

Some psychobabble: Object Constancy. This refers to our ability to "internalise" (sorry more psychobabble) a relationship: to feel secure and loved even when the person isn't around. It's one of the developmental steps facilitated by consistent attachment.

Parents, remember when you couldn't even go to the toilet without your toddler coming to find you? That's because they were still developing their ability to use the security of the relationship when they couldn't see you.

As adults, we can similarly struggle to hold onto the connection when our partners aren't around. There are lots of reasons for this. Some can be temperamental, some to do with how we were parented, or it can relate to trauma and separation as a child. Whatever the reason, to use our earlier metaphor, it's a "crack in the bowl".

The problem with the "needy" description is that it places the problem squarely at the other person's feet. Starting from a different perspective, there is no such thing as a needy person, there is simply one person with needs, and one person who isn't meeting them. The problem belongs to the relationship, not just one person.

This comes back once more to validation. Being called "needy" is a form of invalidation. Instead, if we approach it as a problem the relationship needs to solve, the task is for both parties to set aside defensiveness, and work to better understand what we might be doing or not doing to meet our partner's needs. Hopefully then both parties can develop the ability to better manage their own needs, and better manage the others. And in doing so we grow the size of the bowl.

One of the trickiest mismatches though can be in the bedroom.

There's no shortage of advice about how frequently we should be having sex, what kind of sex and with whom. Stories and columns abound on the topic because we're all hardwired to be at least slightly obsessed with it.

But like everything in relationships, the reality isn't as simple. There is no right number of times a week to fix a marriage. Libido and desire fluctuate for all of us, from day-to-day, year-to-year and over the course of life. And it's not unusual for our desire for sex to be out of step with our partner's — especially during big transitions like having children and all the demands that come with being a parent. Or as we age and respond differently to the natural processes of growing older (which doesn't automatically mean less sex, by the way). For the young, even the idea that our parents — or grandparents — are still having an active sex life can be a little confronting. However, I for one hope they still are!

Once a mismatch occurs, it can be easy for it to morph into a stalemate, in that some people need sex to feel close, while others need to feel close to have sex.

Stress, depression, physical health issues, self-confidence and body issues can all interfere with our desire. Over time, this impacts the closeness in the relationship. Not being close becomes a negative spiral. As the old relationship counselling maxim goes, when the sex life is working well, it's about 20 percent of the relationship. When it's not working well, it can feel like it's 80 percent.

To change this, it's generally best to not actually focus on sex — try to not make it 80 percent. Instead, focus on intimacy and building more closeness and connection generally in the relationship. What does this mean? Well, just like you would have done when you first met — make more of an effort to listen, talk, understand and connect.

Spend time together, talk and actually listen, go on dates, increase physical (non-sexual) touch, be casually naked around each other, talk with each other about what your partner does, or has done, that makes you feel loved, supported or appreciated.

Create a positive spiral through communication and openness. And — shock horror — talk about sex. Be clear about what you want, and rather than trying to look for signals — ask.

Because while it can be difficult — or even impossible in the long term — to get our libidos in sync, it isn't going to happen by luck. Like everything else in relationships, it simply requires communication and deliberate effort over time. It takes work.

Whose problem is it?

As we've previously covered, when we feel something strongly enough, it becomes true. If we feel like a failure, it can be hard to accept success. If we feel unlovable, we can believe we will never be loved the way we want. And if we feel suspicious enough, then we can come to believe our partner is indeed up to no good.

Therapists loosely call this projection, when our own emotional certainty causes us to view another's behaviour, usually someone close to us, through a certain lens. The most obvious version of this is jealousy. But sometimes it can also just look like taking a bad mood out on someone else.

Jealousy itself isn't inherently destructive; however, as an emotion, it can flare up even when we consciously know it's completely irrational.

It serves to alert us to the possibility that we're losing a relationship that we value. But if our partner is actually having an affair, we don't think of that as a jealousy problem. In that case, the problem is much more obvious. So jealousy is only a problem when the feeling isn't warranted, or when our feeling of mistrust becomes strong enough to shape our perceptions.

So what makes people feel that they're at risk of losing someone, even when another part of them knows it isn't real?

The old cliché is that jealousy arises from insecurity, but that doesn't tell us very much, because calling someone insecure is little more than an insult these days. But it is true that jealousy arises from sensitivity to disruptions in relationships.

Jealous people are sensitive people.

We learn the subtle and complicated dance of close relationships early in life. Some people are born more emotionally sensitive, and for some, the disruptions that happen in their early 'attachment' relationships leave them more sensitive to feeling abandoned or ignored as adults. For some both are true.

Jealousy arises out of these small disruptions in a relationship — feeling the absence of our partner's attention, like they're momentarily interested in something, or someone, else. The problem with sensitivity though is it can turn the volume up on the feeling. What was a moment of disconnection turns into full-blown anger and the fear of being cheated on or abandoned.

Dealing with irrational jealousy requires us to slow down and recognise that our feelings aren't the other person's fault. It also involves, as with all dysregulated feelings, reflecting on the grain of truth in the response we can validate. The intensity of the feeling, not the feeling itself is the issue. Jealousy may be, to return to our container metaphor — a crack in the bowl. It may be that the response to very real, but subtle shifts in attention, connection, or the emotional quality of the relationship lead you to feel jealousy. The green-eyed monster can, over time, become a self-fulfiling prophecy. If we are regularly upset and angry at sometimes subtle shifts in the relationship, it can drive people away and make that which we fear more likely.

And this is the real problem with jealousy, it makes us attack the person we care about; we blame someone else for how we feel and attack them for it.

Learning to overcome jealousy means becoming more comfortable with feeling vulnerable, working with a willing partner to repair the crack in the bowl, and recognising that the green-eyed monster feeds on fear. It requires us to trust our loved ones and embrace the idea that we have to share them with the world.

It can also be helpful to reflect on what our unmet needs were, what those early scars and disruptions were that allow jealousy to take hold. Because wanting to be close to someone, and feel loved and cared for, is about as human as it gets. We never stop needing that.

Violence and the danger of love

Violence is not love. It should never be confused with it. The obsessive, focussed version of love that romantic myths can tell us is somehow indicative of a deep or dramatic love is so often a sign of something darker, something altogether more dangerous. "I can't live without you," is a terrifying thing to say, when you stop and think about it.

For me there is always a simple test: is the lust, love or demand for commitment mutual, more or less?

Because the danger is when love becomes a desire to control the, at times overwhelming, feelings by controlling the object of our love. People do this to manage the fear of loss, rejection or abandonment. And the fear of crippling shame.

Shame, as an emotion, is, without doubt, one of the worst to feel. It can be as simple as just feeling "bad", but when it's intense it can drive us to hide, and it can also fuel anger. Some talk about shame as being caused by the loss of connection, which it is, but ultimately, it's deeper. It's about belonging to a valued group. A tribe. And for all of us the first group we are part of and develop in is our family. Shame is frequently the outcome of early and repeated invalidation, by way of emotional, physical or sexual abuse. To be treated as if one's pain is of no consequence is to feel abandoned. To be told things that imply one doesn't belong, is to be left feeling shunned. Some describe shame that takes root early and goes on to shape our personality and our future relationships, as "toxic shame". Simply put, this means that shame operates on a painful hair-trigger and comes to infest the very ideas we hold about ourselves deep down as unlovable and broken in some way.

When an emotion is strong enough and chronic enough, we can learn to manage it by taking it out on others. Or more accurately viewing another person as responsible for the situation and responding by projecting and attacking. This is often most dangerous with shame. Jealousy, as we've talked about is one example, and the desire for power and control — for ownership of the loved one — is another.

My first paid job in this field was in a group treatment programme for men who were violent in their intimate relationships. Almost all the clients were court ordered, and almost all of them believed that if their girlfriends and wives did something different then they wouldn't have had to be violent. Helping and challenging men to take responsibility for their violent behaviour was the task of treatment.

At the risk of repeating myself, none of this should be taken as excusing violence. But ultimately, they were all protecting themselves from the painful vulnerability of feeling abandoned and attacked because the shame would be unbearable. So, to avoid those feelings, the problem was projected out, onto the other. Power over others is constructed to protect against the shame of feeling powerless, control is monopolised to protect against the pain of rejection.

Tragically, shame avoidance can have fatal consequences in the form of homicide and for some, suicide.

To understand the terrible power of shame is not to excuse it. To view toxic shame and damaging ideas about masculinity as the root cause also doesn't mean it should be the urgent focus in relationships where violence is occurring.

The focus should always be safety. Those who use power and control should be held to account for their actions, and as far as we can, we should prevent any situation from escalating. However, we also need to develop a greater understanding of the damaging impact of the traditional views of what being a man in Aotearoa means. Because the antidote to shame is belonging, compassion and unconditional love. And seeing little boys, teenage boys and young men as acceptable in their vulnerability and as welcome to express their emotions as anyone, is the long-term path out of the shameful record of intimate partner violence we have in New Zealand, and indeed much of the Western world.

At an individual level, it can take work to assume responsibility and to stop seeing all of the problems in a relationship as being the other person's fault. Violence aside, most relationship counsellors will tell you it's a rare couple that finds their way to relationship therapy and doesn't view the source of the problem as the other person's actions. However, when we can reduce the emotional heat, and let our guard down long enough to be able to think and hear the other party, then we can start to see our own role — and we can grow the container, by growing trust.

I've always hated the old cliché that to truly love someone else, you have to love yourself first. Like most of these throwaway lines, it is too simplistic and ripe for ridicule. There is such a thing as self-indulgent self-love. It's probably more accurate to say that if we hate ourselves, and believe that we are unlovable, then this can be dangerous for those we try to love.

Fighting fair

Anger and disagreement, of course, is unavoidable in relationships, but it doesn't have to be dangerous or harmful.

As easy as it can be these days to proclaim that anger, arguing and raised voices are harmful, I'm suspicious of relationships where arguments don't happen. It always makes me wonder where the anger goes, and who's backing down all the time. A healthy relationship requires ways to hammer things out, negotiate compromise and to air hurts.

You need a strong container first, one that can hold the conflict and allow for the feelings. You also need to follow some pretty simple ground rules, rules that many couples follow instinctively because it was what they saw modelled growing up. No put-downs, no threats, no personal attacks, stick to the matter at hand, and as much as possible stick to "I" statements. It's also a pretty good idea to not sulk, storm off or otherwise behave in aggressive or passive-aggressive ways. Have ways for the disagreement to be set aside for a period of time to allow things to cool off, and for people to gather their thoughts.

However, having said all of this, a good container can handle a bit of unhelpful behaviour from time to time, because of one simple word.

"Sorry."

The ability to genuinely apologise, regulate oneself, and our partner, and to come back together is the real key to being able to have safe conflict. It's vital if you have children, because while conflict can be harmful to children, what's really harmful is the disruption and disconnection that ongoing, dysregulated feelings bring. And when we can disagree, get angry, fight safely and respectfully, and come back together, we not only show our children that it's possible, but how it's done.

Even with the most basic of rules, conflict in a relationship means feeling safe is not that simple. Safety is ultimately defined by the degree of comfort of the two people involved, and the trust and safety they have created together. And in the interest of fairness, what's OK can't be decreed by one party, it must be mutual. And if there are differences in what feels safe, despite sticking to boundaries around safe fighting, then it's likely to be the emotional intensity that is challenging for one party or the other, and so the task over time is to grow the metaphorical bowl.

And it's also a good rule of thumb that in any conflict you should be listening at least as much as you are talking.

Privacy and secrets

What's the difference between secrecy and privacy in intimate relationships? Should we tell our nearest and dearest everything, and if not, why not?

It can be easy to assume — because so much of our culture tells us it's true — that we should expect our partner to be all things to us, and as such our relationship has to be a particular way. But actually, there are no set rules — it comes down to what kind of intimacy works for each of us.

Because while we might want, or even believe our relationship has to be a particular way, the process of being open, sharing more of ourselves and building a deeper understanding over time is what works.

Not being completely open about day-to-day things doesn't really matter in the long run. But building a habit between the two of you where you can share what goes on inside will ultimately make you grow closer. Healthy love tolerates a degree of separateness, but perhaps most importantly it tolerates people being able to set and manage their own boundaries — rather than imposing arbitrary rules or demands on the other.

Healthy love is patient, not demanding. It's respectful of your separateness, at the same time as lovingly longing for more of you. Quick, all-consuming love — that seeks to rush from lust to falling in love, to an unearned expectation of love and commitment, is to be questioned, and likely feared.

Grief, letting go and breaking up

Grief is without doubt one of the hardest life experiences that we are all guaranteed to go through. Much like becoming a parent, it is life-altering at the same time as it is mundane in its universality.

It's also more proof positive, if we needed it, of the strength and power of our attachment system. I recently heard grief described as a learning task, which on first glance seems a little cold. But actually, it's bang on. Grief is so difficult because our attachments are extremely hard to unlearn. And the closer the person, and the less expected or natural the loss, the harder it is.

With grief the main risk is getting stuck — stuck in the feelings, and being unable, or unwilling, to unlearn the love. Unable to accept the change and allow the natural process of grieving to gradually lessen the intensity of the attachment in our relational world.

Death is final. Sometimes it's expected, natural even. When someone in their nineties dies we grieve, but we also celebrate a long life, hopefully, a good life. While it can still provoke very strong emotions, it feels easier to accept and let go when someone dies of old age.

Premature, or untimely death is harder to accept. Whether that be a tragic accident of someone in the prime of their life, a terminal illness that foreshortens a life, or worse still the death of a child. In my experience, the more lifetime that seems to have been robbed, the harder the acceptance, and therefore the learning task, is. The most heartbreaking thing is when a parent outlives a child, it seems deeply unnatural and can feel neverending. Some even say, "you never get over it".

To some extent that is true of all grief, at least for people that really mattered to us. Attachment — love — allows us to build up internal representations of our closest relationships. Maps that mean in psychological terms we retain that internalised mother, father, child, and friend — even when they're gone. At first, while we're still learning — emotionally — that they're gone, it's deeply painful and can feel like we keep remembering they're gone all over again, prompting a fresh wave of distress. This is our attachment system taking time to change, resisting it almost.

Over time, we learn. But it is an emotional task that requires flexibility, openness and acceptance. And of course, acceptance is hardest with things we don't want to accept. But accept it we must, and for most of us, accept it we do.

Getting stuck then is rigidity — nonacceptance taking over, and not allowing us to emotionally learn their absence. Denial being the most obvious, and most understandable version. When people get stuck in grief, it can morph into depression. Emotionally at least, depression and grief are very similar. Grief, however, is flexible, and open and enables change. Depression does not.

The natural processes, and the human-made traditions around grief are to be trusted because they help acceptance. Funerals, time to grieve, remembrance and memorials all have their place. However, in general I think in modern Western culture, and certainly, in Aotearoa, we don't do a great job with grief. I do believe it's changing, but generally we don't allow enough time for it, and there is a cultural expectation that we "get over" the loss of someone. Do we ever "get over" losing someone we love deeply?

The answer is we both do, and we don't. Healthy grief, which moves and flows as I've suggested, comes in waves. Over time, when we allow ourselves to experience the feelings and allow our mind to think about the loss, we accept it bit by bit. And as we do, the waves get less, although most of the time when they turn up the feelings are still as intense. Gradually we feel it less often, and as we do, less intensely. We adjust.

It's normal to find grief can still jump out at us unexpectedly. Anniversaries, special places or finding something of theirs can trigger a fresh wave. But it too passes. We end up in place of slightly painful fondness, and hopefully, the ability to remember and cherish them in our minds. We sort of keep the relationship alive, via the memories and the felt experience inside us.

If grief is hard then we need to lean into it, be more open, and more willing to feel more. If this is beyond our capacity to regulate, then we may need help. A supportive friend, or a therapist, helps us regulate and in doing so, process the feelings.

Relationship breakups and letting go

In some ways death can be easier than a relationship breakup. With a breakup, while the connection and attachment may not be as intense, they are still around — in that they are still alive. Knowing that you can still see them — even if you don't — can make it harder to detach.

Letting go after a breakup, especially from a long-term relationship where kids are involved, can be incredibly hard because you're still required to be co-parents and to that extent keep relating.

When people are breaking up, I often forewarn them that they will need to do it over and over again. Because, again, our attachment system takes time to learn and reset. If this is proving hard, then a clean break can be useful. This avoids the cliché of falling back into bed with an ex or yo-yoing in and out of the relationship. When breaking up is the inevitable outcome, all this does is make it harder because it slows down the learning required to move on.

Co-parenting, however, requires people to transition their relationship into a different one.

Because it takes time to reprogramme our attachment system, when first trying to parent together after a breakup, we can be a bit prone to reacting like we're still together, firing up the dynamic that likely led to breaking up in the first place, and causing each other pain. Strong negative emotions can help us to separate but they can also enable us to emotionally stay in an intimate relationship, even if the practical (and the sexual) aspects of the relationship are very clearly over. Ongoing anger and resentment are still a type of relationship, albeit a toxic and unhelpful one. It is unhelpful because it can block us from grieving, letting go and being emotionally available enough to find a more loving relationship.

It can also be less painful to feel anger against another person than to truly accept the relationship is over and allow space for the sadness. Anger directed outwards keeps us stuck and blocks the required flexibility and acceptance.

So, genuinely accepting that the relationship is over is hard but can be helped by taking specific action.

It's important if you're struggling to move on, to work on disengaging as much as possible. The exception of course is if you have genuine reasons to stay engaged, such as co-parenting. It also means working on noticing when your thoughts drift to anger or jealousy and distracting yourself when your thoughts go there.

It can be a good idea to disengage from all social media, and even block them if that helps you not browse their timeline to see what they're doing.

All of this might at times be challenging and painful, but that pain serves a purpose. To truly move on we must go through it — it can't be avoided. Grief must be felt — like all emotions — to be processed.

Of course, if your attachment is to someone who is also causing you harm, then it's important to get support.

The stereotype of someone repeatedly going back to an abusive partner can cause people to become unsympathetic or unsupportive in an over-simplifying, invalidating way, i.e., "why don't you just leave?" An understanding of attachment and the difficulty of detaching enables others to feel compassion for those who are struggling to do what might seem obvious to others.

Violence in intimate relationships is never OK, but when we understand that our attachment system can work against us when we fall in love with someone dangerous, then we can see, and hopefully solve, the problem more easily. Getting someone to safety is the priority, but understanding that even leaving someone who hurts us can cause us to grieve is necessary if we are to be present for, and supportive of, someone escaping this kind of love.

SUMMARY

- Finding love is not a rom-com. It is a series of somewhat predictable steps, of lust/attraction, falling in love and commitment.

- For each of us, love is what we understand it to be. Our map of love is based on how we have been loved, primarily our early attachment relationships with our caregivers. Problems in intimacy and maintaining closeness can often be understood as reactions to our earliest experiences of being loved.

- If love hasn't been safe for us, then it's vital we understand why and learn to use our head at least as much as our heart when it comes to making relationship decisions.

- The tendency to blame our partners for the disruptions in relationships is a common problem of rigidity. As a result, taking responsibility for our feelings and triggers, and managing those flexibly is vital to a successful relationship.

- In life, grief is unavoidable. When we lose someone close to us, whether due to death or the end of a relationship, it takes time to "learn" that they're gone, and that change process is painful. Our attachments to people are one of the most powerful instincts we possess. To reprogramme it we have to go through it, we can't avoid it or we remain stuck in the sharp pain of recognising the loss.

CHAPTER 9:

How to find yourself — and know where to look

THERE ARE SOME AWFUL CLICHÉS in my profession. Call me cynical, but only pregnant women actually have an "inner child". And needing to take some time to "find yourself" makes me wonder: if you are lost, then who's looking for you?

In fact, without wanting to get too philosophical, even the idea of a "self" that you can lose, or indeed find, is strange when you think about it.

However, we all think of ourselves as a collection of characteristics, bundled together to make up a "self". Some of these characteristics we feel are unique, while in other respects we are similar, enabling us to feel part of wider groups. For most of us, our sense of self feels like it emerges from within us in the form of our thoughts, feelings, beliefs and desires.

As we grow, who we become is shaped by the world, and moulded by the cultural rules and conventions we come to live by. But we retain that sense of ourselves as being self-directed and unique.

That creative, expressive self is most precious — because it is still growing and forming — in small children.

Self-psychology is a body of knowledge within psychotherapy that looks at what happens when this process — to develop what we call the "true self" — doesn't go so well.

By now you're familiar with the idea of invalidation, and in families where the needs of children are neglected and invalidated, their creativity, thoughts, feelings and desires are ignored — often because the adults are too wrapped up in their own needs. The child in this situation can come to look to the adult as the sole source of information about how to behave and in so doing neglect themselves.

This self-neglect can be caused by obvious things like excessive criticism and punishment, or violence and trauma. Or the reasons can be more subtle, such as when the parent is lost to such things as depression, parental conflict or addiction, leaving the child to care for the parent's emotional needs.

In the end, the expression of the self is pushed aside in favour of what we call a "false self". This is a sense that our life is a performance, orchestrated by others' needs, where our own needs are ignored, or simply not known. In this situation, a pervasive sense of hollowness or frustration can take hold. It can look like depression, and an absence of meaning.

If this is the consistent experience in childhood, the false self becomes the default. The true self has been lost.

Knowing where to look for it, however, is easy. Knowing how to look, is harder.

Ultimately, to come to know ourselves, at age 4 or 54, we need space, permission and the genuine caring interest of another person. Of course, to throw off the false self, with its weight of the expectations of others, requires effort, but to better know one's true self requires patience and compassion.

So, like most clichés there's truth in it. To find ourselves is to simply connect with ourselves: our deepest thoughts, feelings, beliefs and desires. And to do so despite the fear it may cause.

It also means being able to observe the kind of relationship we have with ourselves, and like any relationship, a big part of that is communication — how we talk to ourselves.

The relationship we have with ourselves and "self-talk"

There is an old saying, that "talking to yourself is the first sign of madness". Personally, I find it's the only way to guarantee intelligent conversation. Either way, we may not all do it out loud, but in our own heads we all talk to ourselves.

Therapists have a great way of making up labels that state the obvious: we call it "self-talk". It's that burble of chatter that's going on inside our heads whether we're aware of it or not. When I was trained, we would talk about the "tape" running in your head, but these days we should probably describe it as the "playlist" in our head.

So, it's human and normal: but what is it that you say to yourself, and how do you say it?

The way we talk to ourselves, kindly or not, defines the quality of the relationship we have with ourselves. At the risk of getting too philosophical, it is us. But for people who suffer from depression and anxiety this dialogue can feel like a runaway train of fear and self-hate.

We call this "rumination", or getting stuck on negative and distressing playlists.

While saying, "you think too much," is never a helpful thing to say to someone who is depressed, it's largely true.

In people who experience depression, the parts of the brain responsible for emotions and for "cognition" (or thinking) and rumination specifically, have more connections to each other than normal: emotions trigger repetitive, runaway thinking.

Once again, pointing out the obvious, at least to anyone who has experienced depressive rumination.

Getting to know ourselves better, then, can be trying when we aren't very good company. And it can feel impossible if simply being with ourselves, in those quiet moments when we aren't busy or distracted, is painful. One of the ways we can experience that pain is what many people describe as boredom.

In defence of boredom

I've always been intrigued by boredom. In a world surrounded by wonder, and so many things one could do, how and why does boredom happen? What does it even mean to be bored?

Hard to describe, but we all know it. Listless, devoid of ideas, feeling as if there is nothing to do or nothing we want to do, boredom can be hard to shake off once it arrives. However, in the space that boredom thrives, also comes creativity.

Yet when we have children we rush so quickly to entertain them out of convenience: handing them a phone or a tablet when we need them settled when out, or out of necessity enrolling them in action-packed school holiday programmes because understandably, both parents need to work. The opportunities for boredom — unstructured time — are increasingly squeezed out of our lives. We also tend to increasingly avoid the prospect of boredom largely via that little bundle of technology in our pockets.

When was the last time you felt bored? The last time you stood in a queue or at a bus stop and didn't get your phone out after just a few moments of waiting?

Has boredom become a lost art?

I also wonder if one of the other reasons mindfulness has become so popular is because it is a way of packaging up and marketing "not doing" in the guise of doing something. "What are you doing?" — "I'm meditating."

Perhaps in addition to meditating, we should recover the lost art of allowing ourselves to do nothing — to ignore that impulse to pull out our phone as soon as we are at a loose end. To simply sit, be with ourselves and reflect. To get bored.

And if that seems terrifying, then ask yourself why? When did you become such bad company for yourself?

Take a break from the screens in your life. Let yourself run out of things to do.

What you might find, is more of yourself.

There is no "self"

Back to Donald Winnicott (the psychotherapist I referred to earlier who said parenting just needs to be, on average, "good enough"), another oft-quoted piece of wisdom from the good doctor is, "there is no such thing as a baby . . . a baby alone doesn't exist". What he was highlighting, in 1940s England, was that we exist only in relationships, and of course nowhere is this more obvious than in our earliest days of life. But it remains true throughout life.

Western culture, steeped in capitalist, free market, free-speech thinking and philosophies is very quick to identify the self, the individual, or the citizen as the unit of economic measure. Margaret Thatcher made this explicit in her famous quote, perhaps unconsciously referencing Winnicott:

". . . there's no such thing as society. There are individual men and women and there are families. And no government can do anything except through people, and people must look after themselves first."

Individualism, par excellence. Well, she may have had a point, but psychologically we don't exist without others, in that much of how we see ourselves is defined in relationships with our nearest and dearest, and in the way we fit — or don't — into our wider social matrix.

Looking for yourself in isolation, even though you may feel compelled to do so, doesn't work. We are defined in relationships, and how we relate to others is our identity. There is no self without another and the idea that we must be self-sufficient, self-assured, have high self-esteem and find ourselves is frankly misleading. Because while a rich and stable internal world is a very worthwhile aim, and may even be one of the best measures of mental and emotional health, the focus in many Western cultures on being a separate person is just not how we work as a species. This might sound like I'm starting to contradict myself, in that an over-focus on being the person others need us to be has been described as a problem, of creating a false self. But in reality, it's always a balance, an endless dance of our own and others' needs.

Other people are also invaluable when it comes to learning about ourselves. Of course, self-reflection is useful, necessary even, but when psychotherapists talk about something being "unconscious" it is other people that are needed to help us make it conscious. This is not a sign of pathology, or there being something wrong, necessarily. We all have aspects of ourselves and our behaviour we're uncomfortable with, and we all have a myriad of ways, usually involving some form of mental gymnastics, of hiding those aspects of ourselves from others. Feedback from others is one of the ways we find those parts of ourselves, and it's usually easier to hear challenging feedback from people we love and trust.

Freud famously described dreams as, "the royal road to the

unconscious" and I'm sure he was right, but in my experience it's relationships that provide the expressway to the unconscious. In the same way, there is no self without others, there is no self-knowledge without feedback from others.

Gut instincts

"Trust your gut." What does that actually mean? Do you think of yourself as someone who follows your instincts? Do you feel you have good instincts or not?

To me, instincts are a great practical example of how knowing ourselves better — our thoughts, feelings and reactions — can be helpful. Often people will arrive in therapy with the idea that there is something wrong with their instincts, when in fact what they're doing is not listening to their instincts, they're simply repeating what is familiar — and that's a very different thing.

Instincts are a particular kind of knowing, described by some as wisdom, deep knowing or trusting yourself. Some have described it as an experience of thoughts and feelings coming together in a synthesis that amounts to more than the sum of its parts, a one-plus-one-equals-three type scenario. It's interesting that linguistically we describe them as being in the gut, because while the majority of our neurons that make up what we think of as our brain resides in our head, there are major neuronal connections down into the body that connect to the heart and — you guessed it — the gut. They are significant enough that some contend they should be thought of as part of the brain. And of course, the gut and the heart are often used to describe particular emotional feelings and experiences: broken hearts, butterflies in the stomach, felt like a punch in the guts, etc.

Recently I had to consider an opportunity that seemed like a good idea, because it was, and yet there was something that just didn't sit right about it. And I felt that in my gut. I liked the idea, was emotionally attracted to it, and it made rational sense. Yet as I sat with it, the gut feeling became clearer — I needed to not take up the opportunity, and so I didn't. I don't know if it was — objectively — the "right" decision, but it felt right for me and still does.

This highlights one of the most important aspects of listening carefully to oneself — space. Our emotions tend to take us towards things that seem like a good idea in the moment, that's what impulsivity is. And most of us can rationally talk ourselves into, or out of, things if we try hard enough. Yet our instincts are often clear despite both our thoughts and feelings but require space, time and a bit of calm reflection to become clear. It also requires an environment in childhood — both inside and outside the home — that is validating. One of the ways to understand the impacts of invalidation, including abuse and neglect, is that it teaches us not to trust our instincts, to ignore the part of ourselves that tells us something is wrong. Invalidation teaches us to stop listening to ourselves, our version of reality as we experience it, and instead to allow our reality to be defined by someone — or something — else. I don't believe our instincts go away though, we just stop listening to them, and in doing so we neglect one of the most important pieces of data for making good decisions for ourselves. And one of the ways of defining who we are is by the decisions and choices we make — what we prefer and what we avoid. And what we love.

Passion and engagement — you are what you love

What are you into, and how do you know you're into it? What do you feel driven to spend your time doing, and what do you avoid? What do you choose to spend any discretionary income you're lucky enough to have on?

All these things, and more, tell you and others something about who you are. And if your activities and interests involve other people, it also tells you something about the kind of people you're likely to like — because they're likely to be like you.

I remember making an important career decision in my first year at university. I had enrolled in a double degree — Arts and Commerce — because I wanted to study Psychology, but I was also advised to do a commerce degree because my best marks were in economics. So I was sitting one day in a large lecture theatre where I had two back-to-back classes, first a commerce paper, then an arts paper, and as I watched the commerce students file out, and the arts students file in, I remember thinking to myself, "those aren't my people, these are my people". Not long after that I dropped out of the commerce degree, majored in psychology, and eventually became a psychotherapist.

To be able to connect with what we're passionate about, interested in or otherwise desire, we also need space, quiet and the ability to go inwards and listen to ourselves. It's a fundamentally creative process, and as such, we can learn about how to do this from theories around play creativity, and high-performance sports — which is also a form of play, play under pressure if you will.

Broadly speaking, anxiety is the opposite of play. To play we must be safe and able to express ourselves freely, without fear of attack, put down or criticism. Creativity and passion come from within, and the ability to "express ourselves" — as the sports psychologists describe it — requires focus and for us not to be in a state of overwhelm. Simply put, it requires us to be having fun.

The concept of flow is a pretty good map for what this kind of purposeful play looks and feels like. Flow is the mental state we are in when we are fully in the moment, absorbed in what we are doing, with no part of our conscious mind unoccupied. The sorts of examples given are often performing music, surfing, skiing, or being fully drawn into a good book. It requires a balance of enjoyment and challenge. Driving, on our daily commute for instance, is unlikely to put us in a state of flow, as we are likely to at least in part be on autopilot, driving, while part of our attention wanders to the day ahead. In contrast, driving a car on a racetrack at the edge of our ability requires us to be in a state of flow, otherwise we risk being in a state of crash.

We can't live in a state of flow, and even with things we truly love we may only dip in and out of this state, but it provides a useful signpost towards the things we are naturally drawn to, and also how to intentionally seek out things that provide us with that kind of experience — a deep joy borne of play and creativity.

Unfortunately, trauma, anxiety, and an over-reliance on rigid control behaviours can, for some of us, make play feel unfamiliar or impossible. I will often ask clients who are parents if they are — or were — able to play with their young children. If they can't it's an important indicator that their flexibility — the ability to express, and be spontaneous — is curtailed, and the ability to engage in flow activities is likely going to need to be a part of therapy. Mindfulness helps, in that it builds the capacity to let go and allow our mind and thoughts to just flow without judgement, as does the encouragement to treat therapy as an opportunity to just speak freely about whatever is on one's mind.

Adolescence and idols

Do teenagers still have posters on their walls? I hope so. Mine were a mixture of rugby players, guitarists from metal bands and super cars. Pretty standard boy stuff. Adolescence is a time when our sense of ourselves is forming. Psychologically speaking, it's up there with the first three years in terms of its influence on the rest of our life. In adolescence the self becomes more flexible as we "try on" and explore who we want to be. Sometimes I will ask clients what they wanted to be when they grew up, perhaps a better question would be *who* they wanted to be.

From Beatlemania to wanting to be an All Black, sadly it's possible to belittle the fandom of teens. To see it as a waste of time, a distraction from the somehow urgent task of growing up, getting an education, and a job. But aspiring to be like someone we admire reveals a lot about us, and the kinds of idols we accept can also tell us about the kinds of cultural biases we have. Consider the different ways we might view a 14-year-old boy wanting to be the next Beauden Barrett (rugby All Black), versus a no less obsessed 14-year-old girl who lives for everything Lady Gaga does. Perhaps the judgements that form around whether either is "realistic" distracts from the fact that having such idols is a healthy and necessary part of growing up and forming who we are — and as such does need not be taken literally.

The same can be said for the clichéd teenage tendency to dye your hair blue, grow it long, cut it all off, wear all manner of outfits, and suddenly become passionate about political causes, all of which can be quite an adjustment for many parents. Trying things on, literally and metaphorically, to find out who we are and how we want to be in the world is vital. And yes, of course, this needs to be balanced with a pragmatism, and we also need to learn how to work with the mainstream expectations of schools, jobs and the world at large. But this kind of expressiveness needs to be seen for what it is — a healthy version of play — playing at being. Allowing a safe space for this kind of exploration of self, as opposed to working with rules when you need to, is an important balancing act for parents of teens, and not to be feared. As I've already encouraged, it can be useful to remember what the world looked like, and how you wanted to be, when you were their age.

And, I would hasten to add, it's also never too late. If for whatever reason you feel you missed out on this period of (healthy) self-experimentation, then perhaps you may want to give it a go? Perhaps you feel there is a frustrated teen inside of you?

That might mean challenging yourself in small ways, changing your appearance, what you wear or how you present to the world. It might also mean having the courage and flexibility to change careers, try new hobbies or explore different activities or causes.

And if you feel you've never quite found your "tribe" don't give up. Finding people who are like us, and who share our values and views on the world, is a deeply validating experience. Figuring out who we are requires us to find people that are like us — being ourselves is always easier when we're not on our own.

Unacceptable identities

Until now we've largely considered the idea of validation or invalidation of the self in the context of our early family experience, and more widely the impact of trauma and neglect. But what happens when the wider society is invalidating us? What happens if who we are, what we are and how we wish to be is seen as unacceptable to the world at large?

Personally, I hate the phrase "identity politics" almost as much as I hate "political correctness". Both are invented phrases that are increasingly used by people to justify their prejudice and hate — a way of attacking something important.

It's particularly ridiculous because all politics is about identity. It's not a stretch to say all of life is. Our identity — how we define ourselves — and the groups we are part of as a result, are integral to our psychological wellbeing and social functioning.

Sadly, human history is replete with examples of the cruel and deadly ways we have decided who it is acceptable to be. Racism, slavery, the subjugation of women, of those with intellectual or physical handicaps. It was only made "legal" to be homosexual in New Zealand in 1986 via the Homosexual Law Reform Bill, which decriminalised sex between men over the age of 16. When first introduced in 1840 the law made homosexual acts punishable by death.

In some parts of the world today, this is, barbarically, still the case.

Racism, despite the best efforts of so many, is still alive and well. And of course, you can't pay attention to modern culture without noticing that gender identity is the current battle for people to simply be themselves.

I should be very clear, these kinds of challenges to one's identity are not my experience. I am about as straight, vanilla, white, cisgender, heterosexual male as it comes. Pretty boring stuff really. Through the luck of birth and genetics, my biological sex (how I was born), my gender identity (how I experience myself as male, female or something else) and my sexual attraction (who I want to have sex with) all line up. And, for most people this is true. If it isn't true, then the odds are in our current world, it is going to have an impact on your mental health. Sadly, it's easy to identify those communities that are most impacted by cultural invalidation. It's represented very clearly in statistics such as levels of addiction, self-harm, suicide and mental illness. It's shown in the known negative impacts of chronic invalidation.

Around the world, indigenous people are overly represented in all of these impacts, as are pretty much any marginalised or minority group you can think of. The impacts are real, and when you view it through the lens of invalidation, it makes complete sense. To be told via the media, the views of various famous or high-profile people, or your church, that who you fundamentally are as a person is wrong or bad, is about as soul-destroying as it gets. The maddening thing is that the colour of your skin, who you want to have sex with, or the gender you believe yourself to be, is not something you choose, nor is it something that impacts anyone else.

When it comes to sexuality and gender identity, it's frankly no one else's business.

This isn't "woke nonsense". When we debate the "idea" of something such as gender identity, we are doing so from the privilege of looking from the outside in, and we are actually debating the right for someone else to exist. The fact that a debate even exists is — in and of itself — harmful and invalidating.

Change is hard, and there is little question that in general, in the Western world, and certainly in our little corner of the world here in Aotearoa, we have on average become more tolerant and more open to difference. Without excusing racism, bigotry and transphobia, I also get that for some people keeping up with change is hard, even threatening to their view of the world. Becoming closed and rigid is a natural response to threat, and one I will explore in some depth later in this book.

If you see yourself as someone who is marginalised, then you will simply know what I'm talking about from your experience. Everything I've said so far about upbringing and validation is true, but even if you've had a "good enough" family experience it's still challenging to navigate a world that at times feels like it doesn't want you. Finding your tribe is even more vital. Being with people who share your experience in some way becomes a matter of survival for some, and of course, this can further make those who struggle with difference uncomfortable.

Equally, most reasonable people don't argue openly in favour of the need for racial segregation or removing the franchise from women. We understand that beating children is wrong and if it happens, we seek to prosecute, and hopefully help, those who act out in such ways. If you hold strong views about sexuality, race or gender identity, perhaps it's time to also recognise that your views can cause harm. Again, this isn't woke culture war nonsense. This is a needed cultural change and we're in the middle of it. Make sure you're doing all you can to help, not hinder others' fight to be who they are. You might just save their life.

SUMMARY

- How we feel about ourselves, and who we feel ourselves to be, is about the relationship we have with ourselves — a relationship that is rooted in our experiences of how others relate to us.
- We experience the relationship we have with ourselves in the quiet moments, in how we talk to ourselves — our "self-talk".
- However, to really understand who we are, we need other people. Objectivity about ourselves is impossible, and we need others to help us see and understand the parts of ourselves we are blind to.
- Validation helps us to express ourselves, and understand ourselves through our actions, thoughts, feelings and opinions. What we feel passionate about, and what we desire are important aspects of how we see ourselves.
- Society also invalidates — based on the colour of our skin, our sex, gender identity, sexual orientation, age and class. Minority groups suffer higher rates of mental distress and suicide for this reason — to invalidate someone for who they are is to crush their belief in their right to exist.

CHAPTER 10:

Are we getting angrier?

THERE'S LITTLE DOUBT THAT over my lifetime the world has come to feel angrier. Perhaps it's the impact of social media, the ability for everyone and anyone to have a platform where they can share their views at any time to the whole world. Maybe it's the growing global stress of climate change, and more recently the global pandemic with its various public health interventions that have upset so many.

Perhaps it's more accurate to say polarisation has increased. Us versus them, Republican or Democrat, Left or Right, Free Speech or Cancel Culture, Vaxxed or not, Climate Change or Climate Denier. It feels like the world has become a series of teams that we all must pick from. And look out if you pick the wrong one!

It's possible of course that we aren't angrier, that what we're seeing has to some extent always been there, but now with the fast-paced nature of media, and our wired lives via the amazing super computers that live in our pockets, we're more aware of it and more able to hear about it. Is technology the cause, or merely the messenger?

I'm not a technology hater, in fact for a late Gen X-er (or is it Xennial?) I love it all. I'm online, and use social media a lot. I spend most of my social media time on Twitter — perhaps the angriest of all mainstream online platforms.

Partly because I see it as a bizarre, twisted, real-time psychological experiment, and partly because I actually have real, genuine people who I connect with there. It's not all bad. But when it is bad, and this applies to modern culture offline as well as online, it can be very bad.

As you're now familiar with, dysregulation is the term for a high level of emotion that clouds our vision and shapes the world to fit. Feelings become facts. What's also true is that the more dysregulated we become, the more we tend to fall into what we call black-and-white thinking. High emotions make it harder to see nuance and tend to push us to simplify — good or bad, right or wrong.

And when someone is good or right, then there must be other people who are bad or wrong. Anger of course makes us right; a feature of anger is to feel righteous — and defend our views.

It's a heady mix, and very human. As we feel more distressed, we're less likely to see nuance, more likely to feel right, and more likely to attack. This causes anger and defensiveness in others, who in turn are more likely to lash out, cause more defensiveness, and on and on the rage machine goes.

But where is all this distress coming from in the first place? What is the chicken and what is the egg?

Some of it is just life — and the fact that theoretically we all take our feelings out on other people and have been doing so since the beginning of time.

But I genuinely believe that we are all living through a period of unprecedented change and disruption. And that much of what is fuelling the growing collective distress is the accelerating change, and the very normal response to change — grief.

Therapy is primarily oriented around helping people be less reactive, less inclined to fight — generally speaking.

Anger management, understanding our impulses, and taming the beast within are all valid clichés of the approach therapists take to deal with anger, and with good reason. Anger and fighting can be hugely destructive. But there is such a thing as healthy aggression and there are fights worth having. I hope to consider both.

Collective grief and the modern world

Constant change is the natural way of things, whether we like it or not. Our bodies change, we age, those we love die, and the seasons come and go. Despite the fact that humans want to cling on to how things are, they never stay the same. So much of our existence is beyond our control, but we cling to it nonetheless. This is the essence of what the Buddhists mean when they talk about attachment, and how it causes suffering. It causes distress because we want stability, but largely the universe does not provide us with that. So, we create islands of stability, and we create the illusion of impermeability. We create routines, we build edifices and traditions. Humanity creates stability to soothe our need for the impermeable, despite the howling winds of change continually battering us.

Not all change is bad of course. Good change we call "progress". The post-world war years of the twentieth century were without question a time of rapid widespread cultural change, via technology, and the shrinking of the world via modern travel and live broadcasting. Technological progress, cultural progress, and when we look back now the various protests which peaked in the late 1960's were largely calling for more change, and for it to happen faster.

Now, I acknowledge this is all a very broad brush view and scholars of history will no doubt disagree with me in a thousand different ways. However, the upsurge in protests and attacks today seems to be *against change*. Maybe this is because increasingly the changes occurring don't so much seem like progress as an adaptation to things that none of us want to be happening.

It can be easy to feel like no one wants to be inconvenienced by having to adapt to the ongoing impacts of the global pandemic, or the growing impacts of climate change. Unfortunately, not wanting these things to to happen does not stop them from happening. Denial, of course, is a part of human nature.

Before we go any further, I should declare my colours. I have run for political roles, both for the now defunct District Health Boards, and in the General Election as a Green Party candidate. I am what would be labelled "Left" or progressive — and unashamedly so. My main form of transport is an electric bike, and yes, I also own an electric car. We do what we can to recycle, compost, reuse and minimise our waste.

But our family also owns a seven-seater black SUV — second only after crew cab utes as a thoroughly "cancellable" vehicle choice. We fly overseas for holidays when we can, and I fly domestically for work. We eat meat, and even though probably less red meat than in the past, I do love a good steak.

Which of the above made you more likely to engage with what I'm saying, and which less? And why?

Now, don't get me wrong — I don't think any of the above makes me unusual in any way. If we were all to list similar data points then we'd all appear similarly complicated, or perhaps even hypocritical. Because nothing is black and white, right or wrong. People are by their very nature complicated, three dimensional and inconsistent.

Politics of course is organised into simplistic boxes, the most common being what the Western world sees as Left (Progressive) versus Right (Conservative). Change versus status quo. Or, to put it another way, communal organisation, versus individualism.

Simple categories that also don't map well to the complexity of life.

So, here we are — facing unprecedented natural catastrophes, and a pandemic that has impacted everyone. Distress and resistance to change at levels that seem destructive, and I believe feels different — what many label "outrage". And at the same time our emotional systems, through black-and-white responses to distress, or outright denial when it gets too much, force us into battles with each other — and not always about the things that matter.

There's space for disagreement, and we should embrace a wide range of views and perspectives on what matters: how to tackle big problems, and how to organise our society and its resources. But we should also examine our own motives and check our desire to attack without understanding — simply because a different view is held.

Different of course doesn't include that which most countries would rightly view as illegal, whether it be hate speech or inciting violence.

But we should disagree, and we should accept complexity — if for no other reason than it's inevitable. In part, because the only way of figuring out where these lines lie is collectively, through mechanisms, however imperfect, that provide representation and a voice to all — especially for those most impacted by change.

I prefer acting from and promoting values that are important to me and my community, rather than political teams. In general terms, the political communication folks will readily tell you that messages that state clearly what you are "for" (not against) and what you want (rather than what you oppose) are more effective. By being more positive, they are easier emotionally to engage with.

But just like the individual relationship version, it's much easier to get your message across when you talk about your views, rather than denigrating the other person. And when we set political teams, identity politics and simplistic characterisations of people aside, we discover that the overwhelming majority of people agree on what we might consider core values.

Call me Pollyanna, but I genuinely believe most people are good, in the sense that they don't wish to cause harm to others. As a society we agree honesty and integrity are valued, as is the connection with families and love for our children. We may very well disagree about how to express those values, but we all need each other — that too is undeniable.

And none of us is above reproach, even when it comes to things that we might all readily agree is not acceptable — like racism.

We're all racist

Deep down, we're all racist and xenophobic.

Conversations about racism are deeply uncomfortable for most. No one wants to admit to being "racist". Perhaps that's why the term "unconscious bias" has gotten so much attention. It acknowledges that we can all be swayed by our own bias, even though we don't consciously mean to be.

So why is it hard to care for people we don't know? And why is caring limited by our political views?

Psychologists have studied this very topic since the inception of the discipline. In part this is because how groups relate to one another is so integral to the functioning of society, and in many ways underlies every war or atrocity ever committed in history. The history of civilization is pretty much a history of killing those who look different.

This history leads evolutionary psychologists to believe

that this sort of behaviour is hard wired in our brains. We seem to gravitate to those that look, sound and act like us, and be fearful and suspicious of those that look and sound different.

Social psychologists talk about the "in group/out group" phenomenon, as to how this innate human trait gets expressed. For those that we see as "our people" (in-group) it is relatively easy to generate compassion, and those we consider different (out-group) easy to dismiss, to not care.

We now understand that there are actually very powerful unconscious biases at work, especially when it comes to race and difference. Overall, the research on unconscious bias tends to suggest we are all more racist and xenophobic than we would feel comfortable admitting to ourselves, or anyone else.

Nowhere is this clearer, or more dangerous, than in law enforcement, for example, the extreme events occurring with terrifying regularity in the USA. As a result, research into unconscious biases about race has informed training programmes for police in various states in the USA.

Change is always possible and what helps is to make these ideas conscious, so we can actively change them. And whether you think about these attitudes as unconscious biases, primal urges or tribalism encoded in our genes it doesn't matter.

Being kinder to those who don't automatically feel like "our people" is entirely possible. It just takes work.

It helps to consciously expand our ideas about who we see as like us. It helps to spend more time with people who are different, look different and sound different. Experience breaks down and changes attitudes, as well as developing our flexibility and openness.

It also helps to consciously focus on extending feelings of compassion to those in pain or suffering, especially strangers or those different to us. Many compassion-based approaches to mindfulness meditation do just this.

And if you need a selfish reason: anger, hate and suspicion aren't good for you. Being able to turn our minds towards compassion and see the world through another's eyes is good for us and decreases our overall stress levels.

But we all need to be braver. We need to get used to the idea that we're all prone to bias, it's human. Does that mean we're "all racist"? Maybe it does. And if you find the idea that you might be a little bit racist offensive, then perhaps it's worth considering that ultimately people's lives are more important than your hurt feelings.

Sticks and stones

Bullying is a word that has been redefined. A word we used to associate with schoolyard taunts and the singling out of one child for physical attack is now synonymous with the cruel online attacks that seem to increasingly put the lives of young people, and adults, at risk.

But is it any different? Or is online bullying (as tragic as the outcome can be) just more visible, and therefore more reportable? And how does it drive some to such intense distress that they take their own lives?

Singling someone out to run them down, humiliating or attacking them is as old as social groups, and yet in some ways we are only just starting to understand the impact it can have, especially on our emotional development. Traditionally dismissed (think, "sticks and stones will break my bones, but words will never hurt me") just a generation ago, children were encouraged to ignore it, and not let it get to them.

But more recently, research into the effects of all kinds of "adverse events" on emotional development suggests sustained bullying can almost be as harmful as physical and sexual abuse, and its consequences are just as long lasting.

Now of course we also have "cyber-bullying", which is bullying that can be very hard to get away from.

To me, there are some key differences with "cyber-bullying". The first is that it is much harder to escape. If you're being picked on at school, you can always escape it outside school or in other social groups. The nature of social media means, for those who use it, it's always on. And that makes users more vulnerable.

Many social scientists have also found a gradual increase in "narcissism" culturally in the West, and with it a decrease in empathy. Some believe social media is a cause, and some believe it's an outcome of this trend. But what is clear is that the very nature of social media, with the absence of physical proximity, and the ability to read physical and facial clues, means we all risk responding thoughtlessly online (I know I have).

For all the wonderful things social media brings to our lives, in my view it can also amplify the risk of bullying. It can make empathy for others harder to generate and harder to sustain, and it also makes it harder to know when enough is enough.

Ultimately it falls on all of us to not only protect each other from bullying but also to accept that within all of us lies the ability to respond without empathy. To feel justified in attacking rather than engaging — and to understand that within all of us lies the potential to both be the victim and the bully.

It's also incredibly powerful to be an active witness, and to intervene when we see someone singled out. Of course, it's not a good idea to put oneself in harm's way, but being able to approach someone in public, at work or in the schoolyard is highly effective. Ignore the bully and simply ask if the person being berated is OK. A conversation and a little courage are all it takes.

Hate laws

Human beings are herd animals, and we naturally form groups, whether that be tribes, communities, work teams or followers of particular rugby teams.

We generally see people in groups we are a part of — our in groups — as more trustworthy, honest and likeable, and people in groups we aren't part of — the out groups — as the opposite.

But in-group identification isn't so strong that we can't overcome it, as we've discussed. Looking for similarities tends to help, as does understanding and allowing ourselves to get past stereotypes via the real-word experience of people we see as "different".

Ultimately though, those that eschew so-called "identity politics" aren't saying groups themselves are bad, they're saying other groups (out-groups) are bad. Moreover we shouldn't make rules about how to treat groups, because this solidifies a group identity and makes the problems of discrimination worse by reinforcing differences.

Of course, the end point of this argument is that the solution to discrimination is simply to eliminate a focus on difference. This is easy to say when your difference doesn't define you, and when other people don't define you by your difference.

People of colour, women, LGBTIQ+, those with a disability, people struggling with mental health or addictions, immigrants, and refugees. We too readily define people by their difference from some imagined "norm", and we know that when people belong to a "minority group" they will likely do worse on all sorts of health and wellbeing measures.

Trying to limit how much discrimination gets levelled at people who are defined by difference is why we need hate laws: because discrimination is real, it does have an impact, and there is no ignoring that.

You certainly can't just make the problem go away by suggesting people put aside their identity to solve the problem.

But ultimately this isn't the problem. Hate is. And anything we can do to limit the impact of the human tendency to hate rather than embrace differences must be considered. Because pride about who you are and the groups you are part of is fine. But we don't have to build ourselves up at the cost of others.

Politics aside, that's the risk with all groups. Once we find a group to identify with, there's always another — an out-group, who is "not like us". It is entirely possible to encourage and cherish people figuring out who they are through being with people they identify with, without hating them for it, or forming groups based on hate.

We can embrace difference, and it's even easier if you engage with those you see as different. Because it is both true that we are different, and they are us.

Even bullies need love

Of course, everyone wants less bullying, and everyone wants to protect the victims of bullying. But what do we do about the bullies?

It's natural, as a parent, to be protective. If you find out your kid's getting bullied most of us would instinctively want to wade in and sort it out, one way or another. Talk to the bullies' parents, maybe even give them a taste of their own medicine.

It might make you feel better, but bullying isn't solved by more bullying. You can't bully a bully into stopping bullying.

For most, bullying, or "acting out" with aggression is a sign of distress. Bullies don't intimidate and hurt other kids because they're happy. They do so because it is a way to stop feeling the distress they feel, even momentarily.

And no, it's not as simple as "kid gets bullied by their parents, and then bully other kids". It isn't just about getting yelled at or hit at home, although for some that might be the cause.

It also isn't just a "lower socio-economic problem". Some of the best schools have bullying problems because the unrelenting pressure and expectations on our kids to be perfect is also a form of bullying, or at least deeply critical and harmful.

It's just too easy — too tempting — to see the behaviour as the problem, to punish the bully and be done with it. We do that too easily in New Zealand — punish without wanting to understand — because we think it solves the problem.

But ultimately when we punish the person rather than attend to the behaviour we send the message that the person is bad. We need to send the message that the behaviour is not acceptable, and we want to understand what it is going on in the young person's life. And ultimately, to help them with it.

We need to demonstrate compassion.

For bullies — indeed for all of us — the worst bully will be the one in our own head. That self-critical voice that lays into us when we make a mistake or fail to live up to the pressure and expectations that have been imposed on us by society, our teachers, schools, or our families.

And when we punish the child acting badly, ultimately all we do is give that self-critic more ammunition.

That's not only harmful — it can be deadly.

A nation of bullies

We all have myths and half-truths we tell ourselves, it's what we call an "ego ideal". It's the positive version of how we imagine ourselves to be. At best it's a half-truth, at worst it can be a complete fiction.

As New Zealanders I believe we like to think of ourselves as a nation of "can-do" people, hard but fair, self-reliant but caring.

Yet some studies suggest we have the second worst rate of youth bullying in the world, with just over a quarter of 15-year-olds reporting being bullied at least a few times a month.

This is concerning for many reasons, in large part because we know that bullying has long-lasting consequences. It often leads to depression, anxiety and suicidal thoughts for teenagers and adults.

So, no matter what we might like to think about ourselves, the uncomfortable reality is that New Zealand is a violent country and getting more so. We might not be armed to the teeth with semi-automatic weapons like the US, but our violence can be just as deadly.

Deadly particularly for our young people. Sadly, New Zealand is frequently world-leading in our teen suicide rate.

Our rangatahi are being killed by their own pain, killed indirectly by the violence of others. But it isn't our attitude towards the bullied that needs to change, it's our attitude towards the bullies.

Because we are a nation that loves to punish.

As regular as clockwork, politicians will trot out the "tough on crime" rhetoric. New Zealand has an incarceration rate nearly twice that of Australia and we're building more prisons while our health system languishes in disrepair.

It's a challenge to respond without revenge, to speak out when we're distressed or in pain, and to respond with compassion to the bully — or the criminal. Instead, we must allow ourselves to be vulnerable, to feel pain and distress, and allow ourselves to connect with that in others.

We must see other's suffering as our own.

Somewhere along the way we lost our sense of

collectivism, the sense that as a country we're all in this together. Maybe it's a global trend, maybe it's due to the inherent competition of capitalism.

Increasingly, we all battle on in the belief that as long we make sure we're OK, then that'll do. And if someone else is struggling, then it's not our problem, it must be their own fault, right?

But turning a blind eye is its own special form of violence. And how can we expect our young people to treat each other with respect and kindness when their parent's generation turns on each other at the first excuse?

Going to punishment as a first resort simply doesn't work. It can feel like it works because it feels good to do something, to have a target to legitimately take it out on when you're distressed and angry. But it rarely leads to behaviour change.

On being offended

What does it mean to be offended by something, and how do we know when we are? To be offended is to feel a mix of hurt and angry emotions. It happens when we feel that we, or someone or something we care about has been attacked or put down.

I've talked a lot about validation and how hard it can be to simply allow others their emotional responses. We can all be guilty of telling someone to "get over it" when they are upset for reasons that we don't understand.

Telling someone they shouldn't be offended, is, of course, a very specific type of invalidation.

Like a lot of emotionally invalidating behaviours, most people don't intend to offend or invalidate, but equally, if your response is any version of "That's just political correctness gone mad" then you probably need to sit down, shut up and listen for a change.

Not meaning to offend is understandable, but no excuse. It's certainly not a reason to stop listening and understanding. After all, if someone is hurt by your words, why wouldn't you want to know about it? Is being right so important that you don't care?

Culturally in New Zealand we've always had this slightly cruel, jocular way of talking with each other, especially as men. Taking the piss or putting others down in funny and witty ways is something we will all recognise. But it's a fine line between taking the mickey and bullying.

I don't believe for one moment people are now more easily offended, though I do think it's true we are hearing more about it. It's much easier for all of us to have a voice, whether that is because of social media, or just due to the fact we no longer expect women, minorities and the disaffected to shut up and take the abuse.

Ultimately, this is a good thing. What's wrong with wanting to live in a world where people can speak up if they feel hurt, challenge people to be more thoughtful with their words, and not attack or belittle people because of their gender, looks, skin colour or views on the world?

But privilege is hard to spot when you've benefited from it. Our egos make it hard to see, and even harder to admit.

Snowflakes

Generally, I'm not a fan of generalisations. It's just a short skip and a jump from there to a stereotype, and its evil cousin, prejudice.

But we just can't seem to help ourselves when it comes to age and generations. Gen X, Baby Boomers, Millennials, Gen Z: we all know our place. And almost on a weekly basis, we get told that Millennials (or more recently Gen Z) — well they're a bit special, aren't they?

The term "snowflake generation" was even one of the *Collins English Dictionary*'s words of the year in 2016. It refers to the idea that someone is overly sensitive, with an entitled idea of their own importance and sensitivity. It's seen as the result of a generation that has been coddled and convinced of their specialness.

In reality it is a term of abuse and captures the very worst of the hateful attitudes some hold towards those younger than themselves.

I've talked a lot about validation and the potential that invalidation has to cause harm. There is little more invalidating than writing off the concerns and emotions of an entire generation by labelling them snowflakes.

The reality is, for much of human history we have failed to grasp the impact of sexism, racism, physical and sexual abuse and many other injustices on people's health.

The history of understanding mental health is actually the history of understanding the impact of trauma.

While many still choose to minimise or outright deny the impact of these abuses, we have rightfully raised a generation to be aware and speak out, at the same time as we abuse and belittle them for doing so.

Is it any wonder the levels of anxiety and depression amongst young people in the Western world are on the rise?

Why you'll never win an argument online

If you've ever spent any time on social media, you'll know that irresistible pull to jump into an argument with a complete stranger. "Don't read the comments" is the commonly accepted wisdom. Yet if you do brave them on any controversial article — race, vaccines, or the current hot topic, "free speech" — you'll see the digital equivalent of a shouting match, with generally two camps descending into yelling personal insults at each other.

Yet still, we persevere, arguing our point, putting our case forward. And it seems the most logical thing to simply argue the facts, right? Put forward your case and use logic, links and accepted research to convince the other person of your point of view.

Not only does this not work, but surprisingly it actually makes things worse. It's called the "backfire effect" and numerous studies have shown that when you try to convince someone to change strongly held beliefs, presenting them with "facts and evidence" actually strengthens their views.

We all like to think of ourselves as rational creatures, holding ideas, opinions and beliefs about the world because we've given it thought and reached a reasonable conclusion. But those strongly held views, the things we're most passionate about, become part of us — psychologically speaking — and as a result are very hard to change.

An attack on those beliefs — which is ultimately what contradictory evidence is — feels like an attack on us, and so we defend our views as strongly as we would defend our very selves. And of course, if we then also resort to personal attacks, we have no hope of doing anything except cementing the very beliefs we wish to challenge.

In short: we're all hard-wired to care more about our ego and being right, than the facts.

So, don't read the comments, and ideally don't even try to

change someone's mind via a comments thread. But I know you will, so if you do, what should you do differently?

Firstly, give up trying to convince anybody of anything and try to understand their view first. Ask questions and try to see the world from their point of view. For example, so called "anti-vaxxers" are largely motivated by fear for their children's wellbeing and a lack of trust in big pharmaceutical companies. And most racism is fuelled by fear of difference and a lack of real-world positive experience of those differences.

Of course, understanding doesn't mean accepting, and I'm certainly not advocating you tolerate being abused or attacked.

But try to find similarities, and ideally shared values. All parents are worried about their children's health and want to protect it, whether you're for or against vaccinations.

Feel free to explain your own point of view, and why you feel that way, in the knowledge that it's unlikely to change other people's minds but can lead to a better understanding of the similarities.

By far the biggest problem with the backfire effect is not that it stops you from winning the argument — you were never going to win it anyway — but that it predicts widening differences. The more we argue, try to convince and attack the views of others, the more intensely we disagree.

And while we absolutely should try and understand hate speech, and so-called "alt-right" views, we don't have to tolerate it, and we certainly don't have to allow it a venue to promulgate its views.

Why you should punch Nazis

I've always considered myself a pacifist and have never been in a fight (off the rugby field) in my life. Yet if some things are worth fighting for, are some things also worth assaulting someone for?

With the rise of the alt-right in the USA and around the world, an idea took hold, and at times was enacted in real life, that punching literal Nazis is not only OK but to be encouraged. Some ideas are reprehensible enough that violence seemed like the only response. When violence is being espoused, should we not meet it with the same?

What you're prepared to fight for — not bully, belittle or pile-on via social media — but actually stand up and fight for is one of the best ways to truely know who we are, and to know what — or who — matters to us.

The rise of the alt-right around the world, and its targeting of minority groups, is something we should all stand firm against. But more than that, we should also fight anything that seeks to encourage our worst impulses. It's not true to say that racism is a form of mental illness, nor that extreme political beliefs are a sign of psychiatric disturbance. If nothing else this is an insult to anyone struggling with mental illness. But it is possible to understand the actions of those drawn to extreme ideologies through a psychological lens.

Fascist beliefs, and their racist and anti-difference agendas utilise the dynamics of in-groups/out-groups to make minority groups targets and scapegoats, to build themselves up at the expense of putting other groups down. It is, in uncertain times where it feels so much is changing so quickly, understandable to retreat into rigid, black-and-white thinking. As we've discussed, fear does that. But to choose to elevate one's self-identity at the expense of others is a fundamentally narcissistic strategy, one that is fiercely individualistic, and also low in empathy. A retreat to rigidity to defend against fear is a normal human defence. However to entrench that by building a set of beliefs, and even a political movement around attacking out of a need to feel powerful is to create a mental straightjacket for oneself, to trade reality for a sense of (illusory) safety.

Whether it's Q-Anon or extreme Covid deniers, no problems are being solved by these beliefs, except the sense of community these people feel as they subscribe to these ideas. But it is at the expense of others, and this is something we must always fight — whether it is literally punching a Nazi — or fighting for the protection of truth and the value of consensual reality.

The emotional impacts of modern society are the best compass for what we should fight. Whether it's working to make society more accepting and welcoming for all people regardless of their difference; making society less unequal so we can ensure a quality of living so all can live with dignity; protecting those who are vulnerable, and ensuring those who tend to take advantage of others are held responsible for their actions; or simply making sure everyone can access mental health support when they need it. These and many other examples, are the fights always worth having.

Psychotherapy and psychiatry have fallen into the trap of individualising suffering, of locating the "problem" solely inside the patient sitting in front of us. As recently as the middle of the last century, trauma was barely considered in the understanding of what could lead people to extreme states of distress. The whole language of mental "illness" reinforces this idea, that just like a virus, something is in us that makes us ill.

Ironically, a real virus, Covid-19, has made it clearer that distress is a result of who we are, interacting with where we are, and what happens to us is the result of both. Throughout the initial lockdowns and fear in 2020, people who had never struggled with their emotional health found themselves experiencing distress. While some turned to the false safety of disinformation, many more turned to therapy; to the tools of mental health to manage anxiety, low mood and isolation.

Psychotherapy at its core seeks the truth and focusses on

the ways we shy away from the truth because it's too painful.

Therapy helps us to think and see clearly when the path is hard to find.

Our species tends to shy away from the truth, and into denial. We only need to look at the response to the growing danger of the climate catastrophe happening right now, all around us, or the recent pandemic to see that in action. Our collective tendency to slide into either hopelessness or denial may very well be the undoing of us. However, in that sense, it's not hyperbolic to suggest that therapy can save us, by helping us stay present to reality, and fight for the things that really matter.

SUMMARY

- To pay attention to the news and current events is to experience a world that seems to be getting angrier and angrier. As world events dysregulate us, we are all prone to seeing the world in black-and-white terms, and as a result getting increasingly rigid. Seeing an "us" and a "them" in every disagreement.
- Bullying and attacking others is almost always a way to rid ourselves of tension and uncomfortable feelings. It is a rigid response to dysregulated emotions that leads us to try to control others.
- Understanding that those who lash out are in pain is vital — we won't defeat bullying by bullying bullies. Ultimately, people who lash out require understanding and support.
- For many of us, being comfortable with those that are different to us requires work. Trusting those like us, and being suspicious of those who aren't, is human nature. Exposure to difference is vital in all our lives as it breaks down these rigid ideas.
- Fighting for what you believe in, protecting yourself, and for the rights of others is healthy anger. If necessary, you should always punch a Nazi.

CHAPTER 11:

If life has a meaning — what is it?

WE BEGAN THIS JOURNEY with a consideration of the role of death, and how it shapes so much of our psychological world. As we age, we feel that pinch of mortality more sharply. There is little question it comes to influence and even direct many of our choices — either recklessly in stout defiance of the inevitable, or in a shifting of our priorities and values in the face of shrinking time.

While we can't live for ever, despite religious ideas about how we might live on in some fashion other than this mortal life, human beings are motivated by something we commonly think of as "making your mark" or leaving some form of legacy. For many that will be the task of raising the next generation, and if we are lucky, living long enough to see our children raise their own offspring. Some even get to glimpse over the horizon to the generation after that. But raising a family is only one way to leave a legacy, even if it is the most common and biologically obvious one.

Developmental psychology refers to this task as being one of "generativity".

It's possible to be cynical — or is that realistic — and see aspects of generativity as a defence against the inevitable fear and pain of a finite life. To feel that some part of us, our ideas, our work or our influence, lives on beyond the limits of our life. I will readily admit that writing a book certainly fits that bill for me. It somehow feels good to know a real physical book will be knocking around in the world, hopefully, long after I'm gone.

Remember: it's only a problem if it's a problem. Finding creative ways to ease our way through this short mortal journey is a good idea. Imperative even.

What does it all mean?

I mean honestly, who knows? I don't pretend to have any kind of answer. Ultimately, no one knows what the point of it all is, and what happens when you die. Or whether there is any grand plan for any of us or human life in general.

In the interests of transparency, I don't subscribe to any organised religion. In terms of defining my views, I guess you could say I'm an atheist, but it wouldn't be true to say that I don't believe in anything. I trust science and believe nature is so complex and awe-inspiring that it leads me to believe in natural selection via evolution, and the resultant astounding range and complexity of life on planet Earth. I don't believe anything happens to our consciousness when we die — the electrical signals in our brain fade and simply stop. In a very concrete way, all matter that composes us does go back into nature and begins the cycle of life again. In that sense the physical matter that is us lives on, indeed has lived already since the beginning of it all.

That's pretty amazing when you think about it.

I don't think it matters what you believe, or whether what you believe is objectively provable. Science would suggest that the observable (to us at least) processes of nature are verifiably accurate. But who knows what there is that we can't see, or are yet to know about?

And while it doesn't matter what you believe, I do think it's important that you believe in something. Because without it, finding ways to experience awe can be very difficult — and awe as an experience is good for us in a myriad of ways. Like I've already discussed, this experience seems to be part of what makes psychedelic drug-assisted therapy work. And in general, feelings of awe can lift our mood, shift our perspective, and make us feel more connected to those around us, and to our community. Generally speaking, it is a pro-social emotion, and one which increases our sense of community with our fellow humans, along with decreasing our sense of ego and individualism, leaving us more humble.

The more I learn about awe, and what we might generally think of as "spiritual" moments and grass-roots religion, the more they seem diametrically opposed to purely individualistic, capitalist-driven ideas that continue to dominate so much of the West. Not to mention the inherently political and hierarchical structures that are many of the large, organised religions.

However, for our purposes here let's just keep it to the experiences of worship, prayer and more broadly spiritual engagement — which is in many ways separate it from the more problematic, political structures of organised religion.

At a community level religion provides a sense of belonging, via regular ongoing social contact with a group of people who we can be assured share similar values and ideas about life as us. Religion also provides a sense of guidance about the path to take, and ways to act in a generally pro-social manner (religious conservative politics aside). Think charitable efforts and support for those in need that many churches and community groups engage in.

And, of course, singing, largely in groups.

These things aren't all accidents, and regardless of whether you're a devout churchgoer or someone who has no engagement with organised religion like me — there's something to be noted here about what works.

Creating meaning

There's a particular absurdity about life, which when we truly embrace the idea that it's all inherently meaningless lightens what would otherwise be a deeply despairing thought. Because if we accept that none of it really means anything, we are also then free to create our own meaning — to find what works for us.

And, if we add nature, and seek experiences of awe in the natural world to the list above, then I believe we have a pretty good map for building activities and structures into life that help us feel our existence is meaningful.

It's vital we feel part of a community of some sort. Whether it is belonging to a club, a sports team, a book club, or a community of families with similar-aged children — to truly thrive we need a tribe. A place to stand and know we are loved and valued.

It helps if we come together with like-minded people who share our values or our place in life's journey. I believe these sorts of community collections work when there is a shared purpose, and/or shared values. It doesn't have to be as simplistic as everyone agreeing with each other, or worse still, voting the same way. A sports team or club comes together for the purpose of enjoying their chosen sport and maintaining the history and continuity of their chosen club's identity. Whereas a charity or community-action group comes together because of tasks motivated by very clearly identified shared values and likely even political views. Coming together with those like us in some way is inherently validating, because the validation of sameness is implicit.

Helping others — or what we might describe as "contributing" — is fundamental to a meaningful life. And there are lots of ways to do it. It's not just signing up to volunteer at a soup kitchen, although that's awesome too. Contributing is really just doing things for others, and it's likely, if you're plugged into a community already, you're already doing this. Looking after friends' kids, hosting playdates, helping a mate paint a fence, coaching your kid's sports team, or mowing your elderly parents' lawns. These are all lovely things to do, and if you have strong values of family and forming networks where seamless quid pro quo happens, this likely works very well.

The main thing is to find ways to give and help that match your values, and involves doing something, ideally in person, for those being helped, or as a group working together on a cause. I've not seen any research on the difference between giving time versus money, but I suspect that the wellbeing impacts are larger for volunteering than donating. That's not to say philanthropy isn't good too!

The underlying mechanism for much of this pro-social behaviour is what can seem like a strangely radical idea in today's cynical and negative news cycle: human beings are fundamentally altruistic.

Altruism

If you spend too much time watching the news, or worse reading the comments online, it can be easy to feel like the human race is spiralling towards ever more cruelty, selfishness and brutality.

Yet despite this, at least in day-to-day life, most people

seem fundamentally good. Society in Aotearoa, despite everything, works. Underpinning the capacity for billions of human beings on the planet to live with varying levels of cooperation, is the imperfect ability to be altruistic.

Altruism is something that has puzzled psychologists and students of human nature throughout human history. If you look at our species from an evolutionary perspective, generosity towards others — even to the point of being willing to sacrifice our own lives — makes no sense. Generosity with those we aren't related to does nothing to improve our genes' chances: quite the opposite.

Yet, it would seem that as a result of living in cooperative societies for thousands of years, generosity and fairness in our interactions with each other is the default. An experiment, dubbed "the ultimate game" illustrates this, and it consistently — across different groups and cultures — yields the same results. In the experiment, people are paired up, and one of them is given a sum of money to share. After one round, you change partners, so you never get to "return the favour" to the same person.

The person allocating the money gets to make one offer, no negotiation, and to decide how much, from zero to 100 percent, of the money to offer to the other person. If the offer is rejected, neither party gets any money, if it is accepted, they both get to keep the amount.

What would you do?

Well, the most common offer in experiments is a 50/50 split. Offers too small are rejected, even though it means sacrificing an amount of money. On the other hand, individual selfishness does tend to restrict people from making overly generous offers, but an understanding of generosity tends to push participants towards fairness.

Capitalism and rational economic theory often have us believe something different. It says people will try to maximise their own gains and behave selfishly. This would tend to suggest that people will take whatever they're offered because something is better than nothing and that those offering the deal will tend to try to keep as much as possible. On average, this isn't true.

On average, people are good.

So, while we may elevate those selfish deeds, those atrocious acts, and the problems of the world as newsworthy — because they are — it's important to also remember that all is not lost. Given the opportunity and the right conditions, most people will do the right thing.

But there is one proviso with the "ultimate game" experiment. Largely, these experiments are conducted with participants who are from the same society. It's easy to share and be generous with those we see as being like us.

Go play outside

We have much to be grateful for in Aotearoa, in terms of our lifestyle and the wonderful and awe-inspiring natural resources at our disposal. It would be fair to say the majority of Kiwis have some form of preferred outside activity: beaches in summer, camping, skiing, hiking, bush walks, and winter and summer sports.

And the science is clear — time in nature is good for our mental health. Part of the reason is awe, and the way we can experience true wonder at the natural processes of the waves, the weather or the intricate life of a forest. It seems to be innate to feel connected to nature and to find a deeper sense of meaning from being in the natural world. Again, for many it's often a feature of what they know makes them feel good. I find the simple act of cycling to and from work is a nice mild dose of being outside, and more in contact with the world than sitting in an air-conditioned box.

It's also true that pre-Christian religions and indigenous societies worshipped the natural world via a pantheon of Gods that represented this sense of wonder and worship of the natural world.

It doesn't have to be a three-day hike or learning to surf either. It can be as simple as sitting under a tree in your backyard or a park and reading a book. Enjoy the fresh air, and a sense of being connected to the earth beneath your feet. Find a method that works for you.

Singing

As I've noted, church involves singing. And not surprisingly, singing is good for our mental health and wellbeing in a number of ways. And the good news is the positive benefits seem unconnected to whether you can carry a tune, or whether you ever sing in public.

If like me you tend to sing along with songs in the car, then you'll know that such a simple act can shift moods. That simply expressing ourselves via singing feels good. So firstly, we know that singing along on our own to music has more of a positive mood impact than just passively listening. And secondly, if you are able or willing to sing together as a group, be it via the church, a secular choir or just a good Karaoke session with mates, there is an additional benefit from singing together with others, in terms of feelings of connection and again — being part of a community.

Meaning in work

For many people work provides them with meaning. However, we do have to be careful about the oft-quoted piece of advice, "If you find a job you love, you'll never work a day in your life." Because not all work is inherently meaningful, and nor does it have to be. It's too easy for the above guidance to be aimed at the privileged few (and I include myself here) who have been able to pursue interests, take time to decide upon a profession, study and get qualified, all while receiving a degree of support to do so.

What work is meaningful can easily become a moral, and indeed a classist argument. I would argue that pride can be found in any job where you're working to support yourself, and any dependents. That isn't to say people shouldn't work to improve themselves on their own terms, but I do think that people can easily mistake their solutions — finding meaningful work, for instance — as universal truth. Work also doesn't equate to getting paid. Some of the most meaningful work we will do — like parenting or caring for family — is unpaid.

If, for whatever reason, your work is a means to an end and you're not particularly fulfiled, then pursuing other work or further training may be a great idea. But equally, we can find what we need in other places, and work can just be a way to provide financial support to allow us to spend our non-work time engaged in things that truly fulfil us. And that might be no more complicated than being a good parent or a good friend and helping out our mates.

The golden rule

There is a golden rule, common to all religions and theologies, from as far back as we have written text, which is some version of "Treat others as you wish to be treated."

As a principle, it's hard to argue with, though of course, some have tried. It does assume a degree of universality which some might object to, and it also assumes that we treat ourselves well, which as I've demonstrated earlier isn't always true. But those are edge cases, and as a principle of pro-social and cooperative action, it is a good place to start — even if it's just to notice how we might deviate from the golden rule, and then be curious about why.

Revenge for instance, or arguments about crime and punishment, in some ways require us to set aside this rule and argue for the mistreatment, or even state-sanctioned murder, of others. Yes, the "others" in this case may be people who have committed heinous crimes. But what motivates an abandonment of the golden rule is dysregulated emotion: hatred and vengeance. And a desire for evil to be "out there" — in someone else. My challenge would be to invoke another vaguely religious rule, "There but for the grace of God, go I" or the Buddhist version: find compassion for one's enemies. And while I've argued for fighting, passionately, for things that matter, it's also true that to live in a place of anger or injustice is to live in a toxic place. Ultimately, we find meaning in love, not hate. We find meaning in coming together by finding our similarities, not dividing based on our differences. And I believe at no time in our history has that been more important.

You can't take it with you

Money is a necessary evil. Spirituality has a bit to say about money, and its pitfalls too. Even if, as it is claimed, Jesus threw the money changers out of the temple, it seems organised religion has done nothing since but invite them back in.

It is important to at least have a passing interest in money, and how to use it well as a tool if you wish to live in our modern world. How you do that, how much you need, and what importance you place on it, of course, varies wildly. Some, of course, make it their reason for being alive, in its most extreme form of collecting money and wealth for the sake of collecting it. Our modern landscape makes it hard to avoid those that have hoarded vast wealth, some would argue at great expense to the rest of us. Either way, the story of Ebenezer Scrooge, where we started this book, is illustrative of the fundamental problem with a life dedicated to the accrual of wealth.

I think it's important to get clear about what money means to you and to recognise it for what it is — a tool. Real wealth is time and freedom, not money. There's no question that more money makes you extremely happy when you are in poverty. The difference between not having enough and having enough is vast in practical and emotional terms. But beyond that, increased wealth offers a diminishing return in terms of happiness.

Now let me be clear, all of this can sound very privileged, to have the luxury of a middle-class lifestyle, and make claims about how money doesn't make you happy. So hopefully I can convey the nuance of the impact of money on happiness.

Below the poverty line, money very definitely buys happiness. But as you add more the curve slowly flattens out, with each dollar buying less happiness than the previous dollar until you hit what has been dubbed the happiness premium. Beyond that, the curve rapidly flattens off. To take an extreme example, if you're a Silicon Valley billionaire, I doubt another $100 million would even register in terms of your happiness.

That happiness premium amounts to annual earnings of about USD 95,000 (and of course varies from country to country). In New Zealand, the happiness premium is estimated to be around NZD 130,000 — 150,000 per annum, at the time of writing. Now that's a very good income, but the point is that many who seek wealth for the sake of wealth earn way beyond that — and one wonders how much extra happiness they're buying. The answer is likely, not much, especially if they're using that additional wealth to buy and accumulate material things.

We all know the excitement — or novelty — of gaining a long-desired "thing". A new car, a particular model of smartphone or those shoes that caught your eye in the shop window. We also know that as delectable as that desire and its resolution are, it never lasts.

Some research has shown that while there is a measurable feel-good bump from purchases like buying a new car, it lasts a lot less time than you might think — weeks, maybe a couple of months, but no longer. The utility takes over once more, and you just have a vehicle that gets you from A to B. I'm not sure we can be quite so equivocal about buying a home, but I suspect it's similar if you already own a home and buy another. We get used to our present circumstances quickly, and to some extent take them for granted.

However, there is one clear piece of advice if you're lucky enough to have some disposable income and you want to create more happiness in your life.

Buy experiences, and therefore memories, not things. And ideally shared experiences with family, friends and other loved ones. Because memories make up who we feel we are, and shared, positive experiences are priceless in our lifelong relationships. I've talked at length about how negative experiences can shape and impact us. In similar ways so can positive experiences. Travel and holidays are the obvious ones, and for those of us who were fortunate enough to have family summer vacations as children, we can likely recall those times quite clearly, decades later. But it can be anything enjoyable really. Day trips, cultural events, family time, festivals with friends, a movie night, or just a Sunday drive to a new location.

Because if money buys time, and time is the real wealth,

then investing in connections and enjoyable activities is the best investment of all.

One of the biggest problems with the accumulation of money, however, isn't about how much we have. It's how much the Jones' family has.

Making comparisons

We all do it. We look around and compare ourselves with others: our success, what we have, and where we live. As social animals, it's natural to look for signs that tell us where we might fit with our social groups and communities.

Not only is it natural, but it's also amplified by our advertising-saturated world, making us feel less than or otherwise lacking so we can be sold the solution. Sold satisfaction and happiness — with convenient finance options.

Comparing ourselves to others is not always a bad idea. Sometimes it can be very useful to do so when done in a particular way.

Generally, we get ourselves into trouble because we compare ourselves to people who seem to be doing better or who have more than us — without (as I have talked about before) allowing ourselves to contemplate the messy reality of others' lives.

People can also (especially when feeling down) use comparisons with others to attack themselves: how can you possibly be upset when there are people in the world who are starving? "First world problem", we say as we laugh to ourselves, and roll our eyes. The problem with this kind of comparison is that it is fundamentally invalidating. It says we aren't allowed the feelings we have. It also rests on shaky logic. As I often say to clients, the problem with this logic is that somewhere in the world there is one person who is objectively worse off than everyone else. And that would make that person the only one who has the right to feel distressed.

That kind of comparison requires compassion, not judgement. When we can compare ourselves to those who are worse off, but with a sense of kindness and to generate gratitude, it can be very helpful.

Helpful because it shifts our attention to what we do have, and helpful because it allows us to see the truth of suffering: that we make things worse or better for ourselves depending on what we pay attention to. Ultimately, this kind of comparison has little to do with what others have. It simply means we pay better attention to ourselves and allows gratitude to become our focus. In this sense we aren't even making comparisons, just seeing our life and what we have through a lens of gratitude.

To do this is to swim against the tide. It is to switch off from the advertising, get off the constant treadmill of capitalist consumption, and allow ourselves to enjoy what we have. When we do that we recognise it's never the "things" that we really value.

Anything we can do to grow gratitude is worth the time and effort.

All you need is love

And so, in the end, we return to the beginning of this book. Where we talked death — and your deathbed scene. We don't picture our car or our bank account. I hope you don't recall with heartfelt warmth the pay rises, the professional victories — beyond a passing satisfaction at your life's work maybe leaving a mark.

What we relish is those we love and have loved, and the times we had together. It's almost trite to suggest love is all we need — but the Beatles were right about many things, with this being perhaps the most profound.

Orient your life around love, connection and safety. Build relationships and keep them.

If you're going to undergo the hard work of changing yourself, your habits, your beliefs, views or expectations. If you're going to knuckle down and take the terrifying leap of getting to grips with past traumas and fears that absorb you on the nights you can't sleep. If you're going to stop running from the skeletons in your closet, then I hope you do it for love. And I hope doing so leads to more love in your life.

SUMMARY

- We are all searching for meaning in our existence. It's human nature to feel that our existence must mean something.
- If we work at flexibility and accept that we don't know what it all means and that reality may be inherently meaningless, we're free to discover meaning for ourselves — and to pursue what is personally meaningful to us.
- To feel part of something bigger than ourselves helps us feel more alive. Seeking experiences that stimulate the feeling of "awe" is a good place to start, and often we feel it in nature.
- Being generous, contributing and generally practising altruism also helps us feel more widely connected to community, and provides meaning.
- Ultimately, love makes it all worthwhile if we can allow it, build on it and express it. It's all you need, really.

CHAPTER 12:
Bringing it all together

IF YOU'RE A PSYCHOTHERAPIST, you can't write a book without coming up with a new model. My field is littered with them, in part because everyone does this profession slightly differently.

Milton Erickson, one of the 20th century's famous therapists, and a specialist in hypnotic states, was famously quoted as saying, "I invent a new theory and a new approach for each individual."

This has always rung true for me and has become truer over time. While, of course, there are similarities, no meaningful therapeutic relationship is the same as any other. The bringing together of two human beings is alchemical, it creates something greater than the sum of its parts. In addition to each therapy being different, I think every therapist has a unique, internal, working model for how they see, track, and understand the work with a client as it unfolds.

The following model (or map as I refer to it) is mine and it certainly doesn't have to be yours. It also isn't meant to be exhaustive, perfect or even complete. I hope that it will keep changing and developing because that's one of the things I love deeply about my job: you never learn it all, you never get to the end, and there's always more.

Like life, really.

Introducing the Flexibility-Regulation Map

A map is not the territory, as the saying goes (to convey the fact that people often confuse models of reality, like maps, with reality itself). This map in particular is a tool for thinking, and understanding ourselves, and like most tools, it has its limits. I have no doubt it also has its problems and its contradictions. It's just my map, and I hope you find something useful in it for you. You may disagree with how I frame some of it, and you are welcome to. But when a map helps us navigate our way out of trouble or find our way home, it doesn't matter if it doesn't have every detail — just that it's a good navigation tool.

To recap. We can't control what life throws at us, but we can control how we respond. We can understand all our responses to the "shit" that happens, throwing us off balance, and leading to a combination of regulated or dysregulated emotions, and rigid or flexible reactions. Most of us have some habitual ways of responding to the shit we encounter. For instance, you might largely be regulated and rigid, someone who relies upon control and order and largely manages their distress.

Ultimately, we're all aiming to get back to balance. Over time it's helpful if we can be increasingly regulated, and have a range of responses to most situations, building our repertoire of strategies, and creating a more balanced response generally.

By now you're likely familiar with (maybe even sick of!) the most obvious central theme of the book — emotional regulation and dysregulation. Feeling emotions in a manageable way, versus being overwhelmed and distressed. Calm versus distraught. In control of our behaviour versus out of control.

Most emotional difficulties we face in life can be seen as a direct or indirect result of emotional distress and dysregulation. So, on our map, Emotional Regulation/ Dysregulation is the "y-axis" (the up and down one).

The "x-axis" (the left to right one) represents flexibility versus inflexibility or rigidity. You will have noticed this axis as an ongoing theme throughout the book as well, but lurking a bit more in the background. For me, this is the other key to meaningful change.

Frequently the ways we close down and become rigid, and indeed the need to do so in the first place grows out of the extent to which we must manage our emotional dysregulation. How much distress we face in other words.

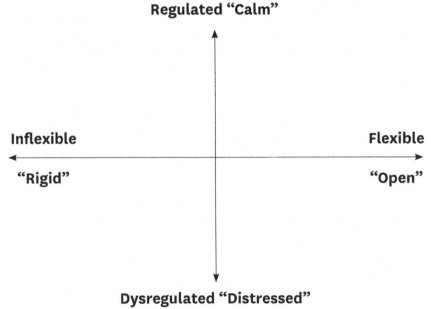

Fig 1: The Flexibility — Regulation Map

Why flexibility?

As a species, our adaptability — our brain's ability to be programmed by experience — is one of our greatest survival skills from an evolutionary standpoint. It's also one of the biggest problems when it comes to trauma, neglect and being programmed by our upbringing, as I've outlined in depth. To mangle the old computer programmer's maxim, "Put garbage in and you get garbage out". In other words, if you put distress in you get distress out.

We adapt to whatever our circumstances are, regardless of whether they're healthy or not. If you doubt how deep this runs, the study of epigenetics, which examines how our genes are *modified* by our environments (there goes the nature versus nurture debate) has shown that famine in your grandparent's generation can influence your likelihood of being obese. The altered genetic structures of your grandparents get passed down to you. Flexible and adaptive. To a fault.

But with any continuum it can be too easy to see one end as good and the other bad. Flexibility good, inflexibility bad. But we all need structure too, just the right kind.

Good flexibility — or effective, regulated openness — is easy to see as a positive. Broadly speaking this top right quadrant is about play, creativity, mindfulness, and acceptance. Spontaneity and the fun of being free of restrictions, expectations and rules (within limits). Holidays, free time, jamming in a band or playing touch in the park. It's easy to see this area of the map as the aim. But we can't live solely there.

Bad flexibility — the bottom right quadrant — (or ineffective regulated openness) looks like being ungrounded, unable to organise oneself or follow structure. Disorganised, perpetually late and messy.

We probably all have that friend . . .

Good rigid — or effective regulated structure — in the top left quadrant is your daytime routine. Set work hours, regular exercise, and the helpful rhythm of day-to-day modern life. All that boring stuff people like me were inclined to say we should stick to during the great stay-at-home lockdowns of 2020 and 2021. Regular mealtimes, going to bed at the same time, getting up at the same time. The reason for this is that most of us find routine and structure regulating. It helps when we're trying to manage distress and helps keep dysregulation at bay. Even when we don't feel like it, we get up, get dressed and go to work. And the very act of doing this, for most of us, most of the time, shifts the emotional state through action. Following structure regulates us, by not following the feelings. We stay on course.

On the other hand, "Bad rigid" in the bottom lefthand quadrant- or ineffective regulated structure — includes hierarchies and traditional structures that persevere out of habit or conservatism, rather than because they work. Placing rules over people, rules for the sake of rules, being right or doing it right ahead of the outcome, and authoritarian structures where just being in charge is the payoff.

We've probably all had that boss ...

Where do you "live"?

One of the main ways to think about the usefulness of the map is to reflect on where you spend most of your time. Psychological theories abound, but one that is a popularly accepted classification — even if it's scientifically questionable — is the idea of being left-brain or right-brain dominant. When you get down to neurological science, it's a pretty shaky idea, but it is a useful metaphor, and as such a useful map that many people are familiar with. Left-brain dominant refers to the idea that some people are more logical, fact and structure-based, while right-brain dominant is seen as more creative, spatial and less driven by rules and logic and more by feelings and intuition.

That's a pretty good way to view the flexibility axis. The

other useful way to think about where you tend to land in the matrix is your general level of comfort with authority and rules. Some people like to follow rules, do things the "right" way, and are generally comfortable with structure. Others prefer less structure, like to be independent or work for themselves, and tend to work around rather than within systems.

If you're someone who tends to feel things intensely or be easily overwhelmed, think of yourself as emotional, impulsive or easily thrown around by your emotions, good, bad or otherwise, then you likely spend more time "below the line". By contrast, if you live above the line, you are likely to tend towards emotionally cool, and are generally not as buffeted by your emotions. Of course, the very nature of our emotions is that they tend to come and go. So while you may see yourself as "emotional" the likelihood, at least in this map, is that you're more or less constantly moving up and down from regulated, to dysregulated as your emotions come and go. Again, the key is to think: where do I spend most of my time? And what do I do when upset or under pressure?

Below the line — dysregulation

Dysregulation has been covered extensively, and it can be easy to again see any form of dysregulation as bad, and regulation as good. But given we all inevitably have periods of overwhelm, we all end up here from time to time. However, it can be worth reflecting on whether you tend to become more rigid and controlled (or controlling of others) when distressed, or do you tend towards chaos when under pressure?

Dysregulated inflexibility can largely be thought of as trying to control or avoid. When we're in this quadrant we're trying to manage the upset and overwhelm via

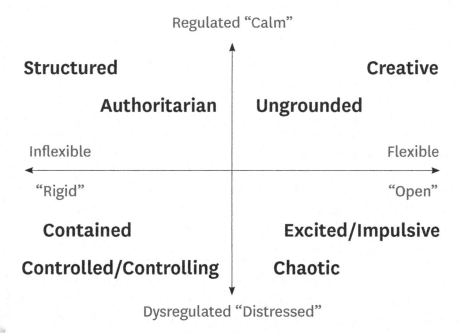

Regulated "Calm"

Structured   Creative

Authoritarian   Ungrounded

Inflexible   Flexible

"Rigid"   "Open"

Contained   Excited/Impulsive

Controlled/Controlling   Chaotic

Dysregulated "Distressed"

Fig 2: Common traits of each quadrant

excessive control and getting rid of the distress. In its worst form, this can look like an excessive need to control others, either to bring the behaviour that is distressing us under control or to blame and attack the other for upsetting us. Either way, this can be benign — "don't talk to me like that" — or simply abusive, if power over and rigid control of others is how you manage distress in your intimate relationships.

If you're someone who contains their distress and rigidly manages themselves when dysregulated this can actually be quite effective, even more so if your desire for control doesn't extend to others. This isn't a great long-term strategy, and people often make their way to therapy because they avoid and control their emotions too much, but it can be effective in short bursts.

The last (bottom right) quadrant is dysregulated flexibility or chaos.

Again, it's easy to simply see this as all bad, much like
it's easy to see regulated flexibility as all good, but it's more
nuanced than that. Chaos certainly can be bad news, and this
quadrant is where impulsive destructiveness lives: when we
lash out, are reactive, violent, messy and hurtful to ourselves
and others. People who live most of their emotional lives in
this quadrant are a mess, their lives unmanageable, ruled
by short-term decisions, addictions, and destructivenes (of
themselves and others).

It is, however, also home to thrill-seeking excitement,
living on the edge, and dangerous but not life-destroying
— or even particularly damaging — activities. Think
adolescence, testing the limits, taking party drugs and
staying out at the club all night, experimenting sexually —
working things out through impulsive action. They're likely
things your mother would frown upon, and while not exactly
safe, aren't going to kill you either. Chaos of the right kind
can be a lot of fun — in small doses.

The up and down problem

In practice, it's easier to locate oneself consistently in one
place on the flexibility continuum than the regulation
continuum because it's normal for emotions to come and go.
What this can mean is that we cycle from "regulated-rigid"
to "dysregulated-rigid", or from "regulated-flexible" to
"dysregulated-flexible", when overwhelmed.

Using the map in this way starts to flesh out how we can
use it to understand some of the common problems we all
face, and how to recognise what's missing.

Take, for instance, a very cognitively smart but rigid-
by-nature engineer (sorry for permeating the stereotype,
but this is loosely based on clinical experience). Generally,
they are structured, and outcome-oriented and understand
things by logically and methodically working them out and

learning the rules. They prefer structure, tidiness, order and predictability. This is reflected in their life and makes them an excellent engineer, and generally stable in their life.

And then their relationship runs into trouble. Their partner begins to express doubts, has an affair, or expresses being unhappy — feels they're emotionally unavailable. Understandably our engineer becomes distressed (dysregulated) — and responds by doing what they know, they use rigid control strategies to manage their emotions. Worst case, they may move to try to control their partner or the situation in some way, trying to get rid of the feelings through sheer force of will. When this person lands in therapy they are likely to want better "emotional skills" to learn better ways of controlling or managing their emotions, so they can regulate and move back above the line. But they're still structured. The judgemental description from their partner and perhaps their friends is that they need to "loosen up" and learn to relax. They need to balance their structure with flexibility.

Conversely, take the stereotypical creative person, who lives life largely on their terms, makes a living out of working for themselves and avoids too many demands. They're generally pretty regulated and have their life set up so that they can avoid too much authority. Then they fall in love, and their new partner needs more from them: they want to settle down, have kids, and buy a house. They struggle with their lack of structure and as the relationship becomes strained, they slide into dysregulation and react by drinking more, becoming less and less functional and more chaotic. They end up in therapy wanting to stop the chaos, but as they calm down and become regulated again, the problem remains. The judgemental description from their partner, and perhaps even others in their life is that they need to "grow up". They need to balance their flexibility with structure.

When we tend to live — for whatever reason — just on one side of the flexibility-rigidity continuum it can look like we are managing at times, but frequently our lives are out of balance. It's like the old cliché — we can't expect to do more of the same and get a different result. We can't double down on rigidity or flexibility and expect it to work. Neither mode is a silver bullet when the ultimate aim is to balance both.

The power of the diagonal shift

Whether it's loosening up or growing up, from the point of

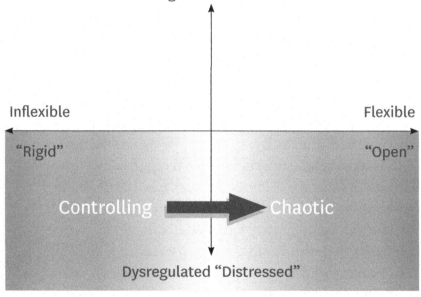

Fig 3: Living below the line

view of the map it's the "up" part that is important. If you can see yourself as either descending into chaos or becoming increasingly rigid in your distress, then great, you know where you are. Maps are only useful if we can figure out where we are, and then plot a path from there.

What I call the "diagonal shift" is recognising that while

much of the focus in many models of therapy is on regulation, and rightly so, we also have to look at how we can balance that with shifts in flexibility. Taking each simplified version of the diagonal shift in turn can help make this clearer.

If you're someone who when overwhelmed or upset:

- Tends to get increasingly controlling of yourself (and others),
- Tends towards rigidity, including but not limited to a need for order, or control — internal or external,
- Tends towards increased self-criticism of yourself for feeling this way including attacking yourself, invalidating and "get over it" type thoughts,
- Has the desire to control how others are behaving, then the diagonal shift is from "rigid-dysregulated" up and across to "flexible-regulated".

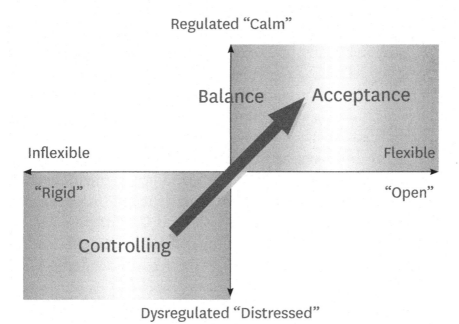

Fig 4: The power of the diagonal shift

What does this mean in practice? It means a focus on developing skills such as mindfulness, self-compassion and the ability to sit with, and tolerate the ebb and flow of feelings and internal experiences. It's what is so succinctly encapsulated in the twelve-step programme's "Serenity Prayer". To paraphrase: control what you can, let go of what you can't and develop the ability to tell the difference.

Frequently when we rely upon rigid control strategies the problem isn't that they don't work — the problem is we tend to try and control things we have no influence over. We're misdirecting our energy and fighting with reality. Trying to control things beyond our sphere of influence just leads to frustration, and trying to control other people leads to conflict, and in the worst-case scenario, abuse.

However, beware the black-and-white solution of throwing one's hands in the air and doing some version of "I give up". This is an understandable place to get to, in that when we rely on control strategies to manage our emotions it can feel hard, and to give up can feel tempting — to just stop trying and let the distress run amok. This can be mistaken for acceptance, but actually, it's resignation, and in terms of the map is actually sliding horizontally across into "flexible-dysregulated" or chaos. Passive chaos.

The key difference between resignation and acceptance is taking helpful action, and in this context, action might mean doing something. Such as undertaking deliberate behaviour to be kind and practice flexible responses. Or it might mean simply choosing to practice feeling without judgement or self-attack. This may not look or feel like you are doing something — but it is very much a task in itself.

In contrast, if you recognise yourself as someone more likely to fall into chaos when overwhelmed, in other words, "flexible-dysregulated" then increasing your ability to use and tolerate structure, and positive control is the aim. It can

be easy to see this as just needing more "willpower" but this
is not only unhelpful, it's a self-attack. Actually, we need to
work on structuring our environment and utilising positive
nurturing control to keep ourselves regulated. Take for
example someone who falls into chaotic drinking and acting
out when they become overwhelmed. It's not uncommon
to say to people who use alcohol in this manner — or for
people to say it to themselves — that they just need to exert
more willpower. Get a grip on yourself — just stop drinking
for God's sake!

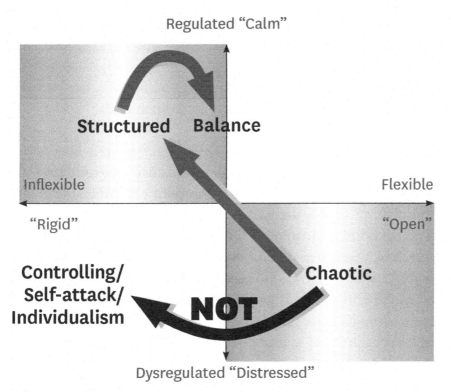

Fig 5: From chaos to structure

This is a form of self-attack, and in terms of the map, more
akin to a sideways horizontal slide into "rigid–dysregulated".
Controlling towards oneself.

The diagonal shift is about moving to a place where you can set kind but clear limits with yourself and work within externally imposed boundaries and authority (that are respectful and non-abusive). In practice, it means growing self-discipline as a practice, not just something you enforce on yourself only when you need to. This means finding rhythms, routines and practices that work for you. For instance:

- setting regular wake-up and bedtimes,
- eating balanced meals,
- trying to keep your home life as stable and settled as possible,
- working to routines, even if you're self-employed,
- setting up commitments like exercise and sticking to them,
- organising your life, managing life's admin,
- working towards medium- and long-term goals.

Goal setting is an important, healthy structure skill. Even more so for people who find it hard, because they tend to be more focussed on the present moment or "impulsive". Impulsivity, simply defined, is the tendency to do what we feel like doing or to allow our emotions to be in the driver's seat. It can be fun and helpful, or destructive and harmful. If you're inclined towards the harmful kind, practising planning and goal setting is like having a guiding star or a clear compass direction. However, just telling someone to be "less impulsive" is more or less the same as telling them to calm down, and never works. Working more generally on goal setting as a way to reduce unhelpful impulsivity is like building a muscle. When we practice it when we're not currently dysregulated it helps us develop a different orientation to decision making, as well as requiring structures and focus that are in themselves regulating and beneficial.

Finding balance

Looking at the map it's easy to reach the conclusion that we should be living in a state of constantly regulated calm, being flexible and playful, centred and monk-like. Just like common misconceptions of mindfulness more generally, this is a great idea except it isn't how human beings work. Life is a constant flow of events, emotions, actions, reactions and mistakes that we all roll with.

The aim is balance and doing what is the best response for the situation we find ourselves in.

That's why I've put balance — or if you prefer a state of rest — at the centre. From that place of balance, we can respond, heading off to whichever quadrant of the map life pulls us to. By responding effectively, we can navigate our way back home, regulating emotions, and responding flexibly or with structure, before being thrown around again by the ebb and flow of life.

Dialectical Behaviour Therapy or "DBT" talks about this idea of effectiveness, as an acceptance-based skill that encourages us to respond in the best way to the circumstances in front of us. Think of it as fluidly responding, without prejudgment and the pressure of excessive, unhelpful rules or "shoulds". It's playing the hand that's dealt to us as well as we can, not fighting reality, while also not being unrealistic. In terms of the map, the more we can practice this, the more quickly and effectively we can return to balance and a state of rest and receptivity.

Individual change

Almost all of this book is about how life impacts us, about how you got to the place you are now, emotionally speaking. In therapy, and change generally, the story — the validating narrative that makes sense to us in a deep way — is vitally important. And sometimes, for some people, that's enough. However, for most of us, there's also the question of, "OK, so what can I DO to change things?"

This map isn't the answer in itself. Because this isn't quite a self-help book — even though I hope it is helpful. Maps show us the way, but we still have to go on the journey.

But taking the time to locate where you spend most of your time can help you target your efforts towards the strategies and approaches that are most likely to help. If you're someone who tends to fall more on the rigid end of the flexibility continuum, then just focusing on emotional regulation will be an incomplete therapy. Likewise, for those who live life on the more flexible end of the continuum. Balance is the aim, and we're always practising.

While it isn't my aim to replace, or create, a new alternative diagnostic framework, it is possible to map out some of the more common diagnoses to direct our efforts when we apply this map to ourselves at an individual level.

This won't be an exhaustive review of all DSM categories, because that's beyond the scope of this book, and would also likely devolve into an attempt to make everything fit. Instead, see this as an exercise for locating yourself on the map, and in doing so to use it to guide your efforts towards balance.

Depression

Depression is a problem of rigidity. Firmly held, often self-critical or (more severely) self-hating beliefs about oneself, that are applied inflexibly in a way that can distort what we see in front of us to fit the self-deprecating narrative we have running about ourselves.

Sliding into depression is to slide into dysregulated rigidity, and getting stuck in increasingly rigid and pervasive, negative ideas about oneself, to the extent that the internal experiences feel inescapable. Claustrophobic even. We call this rumination. Most people who experience depression move in and out of it. In terms of the map, when you're currently experiencing severe depression, you're living in a state of dysregulated rigidity. Over time, especially with high rates of distress, people can slide sideways into dysregulated flexibility or chaos and emotional overwhelm. For some people, this can be as severe as psychotic depression, and if that's you, then the ability to reapply structure will be vital. Some very useful skills and approaches with depression can be better utilising structure to regulate mood. Exercise, sleeping and eating routines are all useful ways to manage the distress and stickiness of active depression, even more so if there is a risk of someone sliding towards chaos.

For most people, depression comes and goes. We move in and out of regulation and dysregulation — the up and down

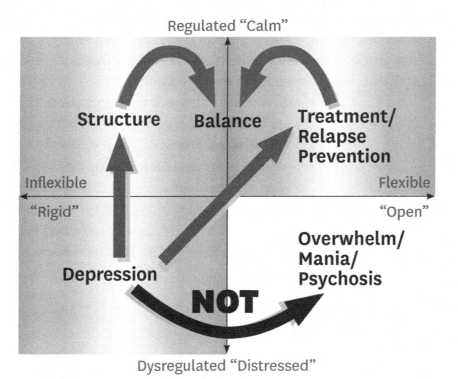

Fig 6: Moving above the line with depression

problem — but ultimately moving away from depression is about being able to hold the thoughts and ideas about ourselves more lightly. To grow in acceptance as we're able to see a wider, more balanced view of the world and ourselves, and overall to respond in a less rigid, rule-bound and "should"-driven manner. Mindfulness meditation has been shown to not be very effective when people are in the grip of an acute depressive episode as it tends to focus people more on painful internal experiences and rumination. But it is extremely helpful for relapse prevention, in that it protects us against further depressive episodes.

Furthermore, recent evidence has suggested that the most commonly prescribed drugs for depression, Selective Serotonin Re-uptake Inhibitors or "SSRIs" may have less of an impact on the serotonin circuits than we thought. However, the leading alternative theory is that through chemical actions, they enable the brain to be more "plastic" which is the neurophysiological term for the brain being able to flexibly rewire itself. In short — it seems that anti-depressants work by enabling more flexibility.

Mania is also a mood disorder, and as it is often paired with depression, and seen as its opposite, not surprising then that I see it as an example of dysregulated flexibility. Bipolar disorder can be seen as cycling between rigidity and flexibility but in a largely dysregulated state. For most people, medication is the primary treatment, and the medication allows us to regulate and find a balance between regulated structure and regulated flexibility. It puts us back "above the line" of regulation.

Anxiety

Anxiety is a bit trickier to categorise, in part because while we might be clear about what anxiety is, it's also true there are a number of different diagnostic versions of anxiety. I'll consider them in turn.

Generally, anxiety is a problem of dysregulated flexibility. Anxiety requires imagination, and the experience of anxiety is one of overwhelm and being out of control. However, some of the ways we can respond to anxiety can indeed slide us across into dysregulated rigidity.

The most obvious example of this is obsessive-compulsive disorder or "OCD", where rigid obsessions require particular compulsions to manage the internal experience of anxiety. Generalised Anxiety, PTSD and panic attacks are all largely chaotic experiences, where feelings are out of control and overwhelming. Efforts to get them back under control are more about regulating the feelings than controlling the experience.

Social anxiety is also a bit of a special case, in that the fear of embarrassment or judgment by others leads to quite fixed ideas about oneself, and again it tends to slide across to rigidity. However, it's increasingly clear there is quite a strong relationship between anxiety and depression, and many people tend to experience both, rather than just one on their own.

I tend to ask people which came first because it's possible to get miserable and depressed — rigid — about anxiety. It's also not unusual to get anxious about — and imagine future distress about — depression.

Addictions

Many people use alcohol and other drugs to feel pleasantly relaxed, and even slightly out of control every weekend. Substance use is perhaps the most obvious, low-harm example of "dysregulated–flexible" that comes to mind. What we might think of as a "big night" in our twenties: up all night, being safely(ish) out of control, recovering (re-regulating) over the

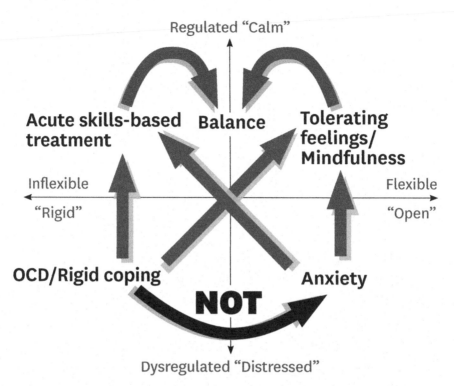

Regulated "Calm"

Acute skills-based treatment   Balance   Tolerating feelings/ Mindfulness

Inflexible   Flexible

"Rigid"   "Open"

OCD/Rigid coping   Anxiety

NOT

Dysregulated "Distressed"

Fig 7: Moving above the line with anxiety

course of a few days, and living to tell the tale with friends who shared the experience, can be great fun.

For some, however, the substance becomes something they depend on, and in this sense, addictions are something that becomes rigid, and habitual. And even if for some their substance use can start as a response to the distress, and feel like a way to manage dysregulation, drugs can quickly appear to be the solution to the problem that the drug is causing. Once in this cycle, we're moving back and forth from rigidity to chaos, all the while being dysregulated.

In many ways then, addictions are a bit of a special case, where the use itself is a kind of dysregulated flexibility, but the addiction is primarily rigidity. It's also true that there are different kinds of experiences of addiction, where some people's experience is more chaotic and destructive, while

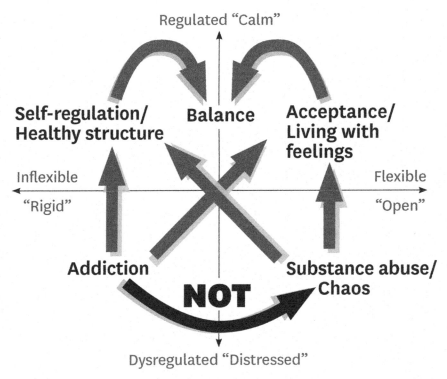

Fig 8: Moving above the line with addictions

others are more rigid and miserable. We see this when we look at different kinds of treatments for addictions. Some people require the containment ("regulated–rigid") approach of residential treatment, where rules, healthy boundaries and learning to follow and utilise structures are the aim — building up regulated rigidity. Others require more of an acceptance-based experience where the aim is learning to tolerate your emotions. Increasing the regulated flexibility side to find balance.

Alcoholics Anonymous does understand and map out the problems and solutions to addiction very well and includes aspects of both — structure alongside acceptance. Responsibility alongside substance-free fun. A balance between regulated structure and flexibility.

Violence and control

As I've stated previously, attempts to understand abuse are not the same as excusing it. It's never acceptable to hurt, belittle, bully or otherwise seek to control anyone, especially those who trust us, like our partners or our children. Bearing that in mind, family violence is fundamentally an issue of control, and as such is an example of dysregulated rigidity. This is a situation where someone cannot tolerate their feelings or allow others to express their own feelings. This means that the problem is projected onto the other (my pain is your fault) and is attacked (I'll feel better if I can get you to stop making me feel like this). While sometimes it is true that explosive violence is part of this picture, more frequently the cause of intimate partner violence is not a loss of control, but an attempt to control others, and to rage about losing control of them. Anger management, and other attempts to increase the perpetrator's self-control may have limited effect, as it's another version of the up-and-down problem. Ultimately being able to better tolerate and be more flexible in response to others — a diagonal shift — is required for long-term change.

And for all people who project and attack, whether that be via intimate relationships, abusive parenting or being a workplace or schoolyard bully, letting go of control and tolerating difference is a vital move away from toxic — controlling — violence.

They have to feel worse to recover, and that is often the hurdle from a therapeutic point of view. The whole point of the project-and-attack is to not feel distressed, vulnerable, or powerless. To let go of the illusion of control is terrifying, and even though people may find this morally reprehensible, establishing a safe, trusting relationship is ultimately needed for change to happen.

That which was created in a relationship and exists in relationships, can't be changed without a relationship.

Society, politics and culture — internal versus external

We unavoidably live in and are influenced by the wider cultural norms and societal rules of our time. Psychology in general, and psychotherapy specifically are often rightly criticised for over-generalising, but what the hell, I'm going to do it anyway.

Even in the nearly fifty years I've been alive it's possible to see that as a society we've tended to slide slightly along the continuum from rigid and structured, to allow more flexibility and individual freedom. We can see the counterculture of the late 1960s as a struggle of a new generation to push for more freedom, creativity and expression after the somewhat oppressive and formal Western culture of the first half of the 20th century.

Fear generally drives us towards structure. It's very difficult to play and be creative when we're anxious and afraid. So, in many ways, it makes sense that through the World Wars of the early twentieth-century authority, structure and formality ruled and was more acceptable — it was the norm. And yes, there are many more factors than this, but faced with the chaos and distress of the World Wars, it's little surprise that relying on traditional structures, following orders and working together was valued, necessary even, for our very survival. Perhaps a need for more flexibility, openness and creativity was inevitable, in the search for balance.

Fast forward to the present day, and the so-called culture wars. The rise of an authoritarian right, the increase in extremism, and the reactions against young people expressing their gender identity, their sexuality and individuality more freely. It feels like the surge for change now comes from the side of authority over others, and control. Whether you think it's good or bad, regulated or dysregulated likely depends heavily on your own politics. Either way, it seems like there is a growing pressure to move away from so much freedom, and back towards structure. From the point of view of the map I've introduced, it is an authoritarian structure, representing power over others, or an imposition of one's views on how others must be, behave and express themselves. That's control, and I believe an unhealthy dysregulated rigidity.

Of course, let's not pretend any society is a utopia of freedom. All governments seek to control their citizens, and even the most liberal, non-corrupt modern democracies have laws, expectations, regulations and requirements. Aotearoa New Zealand ranks pretty well on most democratic measures, and it's easy to point at more authoritarian regimes and see ourselves as free. In many ways we are.

Governments seek to control external behaviour, and ideally, free and fair ones minimise those controls as much as is realistic. Overall, this is necessary. If we are all to live together in societies there must be agreed-upon rules and structures.

Structure makes it all work, and good structure allows for freedom. The ongoing, and rightly never-ending debate around freedom of speech is a good example. There is a difference between freedom of thought, which should always be absolute, and freedom of speech. Freedom of thought is internal, whereas speech is an observable behaviour, which can — and does — cause harm. However, we all need to be able to work things out externally, to be able to say what we think and to be open and flexible to changing our perspective as we learn more. Where and with whom one should talk becomes a quandary.

As children, we all learn internal psychological structures and useful rhythms and routines that are imposed upon us. That's how it's supposed to be, and why parenting is often an awful lot about creating and maintaining those structures. Getting the baby into a routine is a common preoccupation of new parents, and rightly so. Over time we internalise these structures and can run to our own internal rhythms. Children become more and more self-regulating (adolescence aside, as this is a time of renewed flexibility) and settle into being "grown-up". By which we largely mean they are able to self-regulate.

Of course, we also take in the rules of society. That includes clear imperatives, like laws and clear rules, and more subtle versions like social rules — what we generally call culture, or "how things are done around here". In any society, there is a range of views that incorporate cultural norms. Some might be a narrow range, others wider. But it's also possible to discern an agreed-upon level of free speech for example. There will be people who agree or disagree strongly, but generally, people have an idea of what's acceptable, what's harmful, and what's OK to say in polite society.

Too much control over society can slide into an indictment on what we think. This is what we call totalitarianism — or what we might more readily describe as mind control.

In many ways, psychotherapy is the ultimate freedom of speech. "Say whatever comes to mind and try not to censor it" is one of the golden rules. And even though sometimes it can be a challenge, not just because I might not agree with someone's view, but because some things can be terrifying, disturbing and deeply upsetting to talk about. Sometimes, that *is* the therapy. That it's OK to talk about things, and through conversation review, think about and even change what one thinks and experiences inside.

Internal psychological freedom is absolute, and even in times of great torment and loss of external freedom, is necessary, even lifesaving. Memoirs and accounts of imprisonment from such horrors as World War Two concentration camps refer to the need to remain free inside. How maintaining the ability to be flexible and free internally is necessary for psychological survival. We find these accounts amazing and inspiring because under conditions of extreme hardship, trauma and pressure, most of us retreat to structure, eventually giving in to the abusive structures around us. The trauma seeps in, we become imprisoned, lessened in our own minds and institutionalised.

Fear generally drives us towards structure. Anxiety is the enemy of play, we require freedom of thought to create, find a state of enjoyable flow and conjure up something from inside us. However, in the face of threat, retreating to more structure does make sense, even though for those that suffer from anxiety it can be a crippling, dysregulated self-control, marred by avoidance.

In structure we do find safety, in the certainty of what to do we can calm our reactivity, reassure ourselves and know what is happening — even if we have to manufacture certainty to achieve it.

As this book goes to press, we are coming out of — psychologically at least — the intense pressure of a global pandemic. Or at least the government-imposed structures of lockdowns, mandated public health behaviour and mandated vaccines. Extreme measures for extreme times, which in every country they were used also provoked extreme reactions, at least from a minority of the population.

For good and ill, Governments have used fear as a tool

of population control since churches highlighted sins
in religious writings. Fear of war, invasion, cold war and
nuclear annihilation were all "real" but also used politically
as much as anything. The pandemic was no doubt a global
emergency, and a very real large shock — emotionally as well
as physically. And sadly, fatal for so many. The fear was real.
In the early days, I remember watching the news coming out
of Italy and New York with shocking images of refrigerated
trucks parked outside hospitals because the morgues
were overflowing with dead bodies. I didn't need much
convincing to stay home.

The natural response to fear is to hide from the threat,
so when our government asked us to do so, we did. Not
everyone agreed, but it was the most compliant part of the
Covid experience, at least here in Aotearoa. We retreated,
stayed home, followed the rules of imposed structure and
found our own isolated rhythms. Whenever I was asked
for advice on how to cope with lockdowns — and even
when I wasn't asked — I would emphasise the need to find
a workable daily structure. And the importance of getting
out of the house for our mandated daily walks, lest we risk
psychological imprisonment. Balancing structure with
experiences that felt free. Work and play. Rigid and flexible.

Of course, in most countries, people became less
compliant as time went on, as people talked more loudly
about the need for "Freedom". It's understandable, at least
to me, that this would be the pushback. However, where
you fall on the debate about freedom probably depends
on where you fall on a third continuum — individualism
versus altruism.

If I was to confuse matters even further and add a third
continuum to my map — a 3D map! — it would be this:
an individualism versus altruism axis. Both represent
different, but ultimately useful survival strategies, and at

different times we may require both. The evolutionary view is that for altruism to even exist, it must be an extremely useful survival strategy, as evidenced by the existence of an organised society. However, freedom in the anti-mandate movement use of the word was largely individualistic freedom. "My rights" held loftily above all other rights. Vaccines are largely altruistic in practice, because while we can convince ourselves it's useful from the point of keeping ourselves safe, ultimately the more people who get vaccinated, the better it is for all.

Much the same can be said of masks and other minor inconveniences. The fact that some react to a threat with increased individualism, and choose to focus on looking after themselves and their own best interests versus those who want what is best for everyone is an unavoidable quirk of human nature. Although perhaps the vaccine statistics give some clue as to the proportion of each. I'd certainly like to think that altruism wins out if only because I don't think we can continue to survive without mass, coordinated action against such existential threats as climate change and global pandemics.

Some might point to my politics to dismiss this as bias, but I believe cooperation is our species' superpower, and politics aside, individualism is perhaps a necessary, minority adaptation that drives people to do extraordinary things. But ultimately without each other, we are nothing. That is just self-apparent really.

And please don't (mis)read this as some sort of pro-free speech argument. Harm is real, and we should always strive to look after each other. But if it's clear individuals aren't causing harm to others, then each to his or her own. Sometimes that might need to mean imposed rules, even laws, but even better if that comes about because enough of us have internalised generous, kind, non-violent and altruistic structures, as a result of growing up in good enough societies. Made up of good enough parents, raising the next generation.

That's my hope anyway.

CHAPTER 13:

What next? How to put it into practice

HOPEFULLY, BY NOW YOU CAN SEE yourself on the map, where and how you tend to fall out of balance, and perhaps with a deeper understanding of your emotional history, why you do so. You likely recognise yourself in all aspects of the map, but remember — it's only a problem if it's a problem.

So where does the problem for you lie, and what solutions does that point you to?

Let's summarise and consider each quadrant in turn, along with learnable skills from the regulated quadrants that can help you work towards balance. This is in no way meant to be an exhaustive list.

And remember, these experiences might be fleeting, or they may be persistent. Either way, it's only a problem, if it's a problem. But for this exercise, I'm focussing on the problems with each. Think of them as landmarks to look out for as you journey around the four corners of this map.

As you read through each of these take some time to reflect on whether you feel they describe you, as you see yourself or as others would see you.

Rigid–Regulated

- Prefers certainty, facts and ideas to emotion
- Comfortable with hierarchies, authority, structure
- Tends to think in straight lines, logical
- Can tend towards thinking that there are right and wrong ways of doing things
- Can be inflexible about own way of doing things, struggles to accept different approaches or sees them as wrong
- Cautious — not necessarily anxious — but careful about doing new things
- Can be a bit too fond of authority and power
- Can be intolerant of other's points of view
- Looks for information, research and science to understand and learn things
- The kind of person who will read instruction manuals while, or before, using something
- Tends not to be late
- Finds the structure of regular hours and schedules calming
- Naturally uses weekly diaries or planning to manage time and workload
- Prefers a tidy and well-organised external environment and home, struggles to tolerate mess, clutter and disorder
- Can be a bit controlling, even if aware of it
- Can lack spontaneity
- Can be ruled by "shoulds" how things should be, rather than how they are

Flexible–Regulated

■ Tends towards being creative
■ Open to trying new things
■ Spontaneous, described by others as fun
■ Tends to learn more from experience and doing than reading or formal learning
■ Aware of feelings and tends to follow feelings and emotions, to a fault
■ Goes with what feels right
■ Will ignore or bend rules if it suits or if they don't make sense
■ Dislikes authority when it's authority just for the sake of it
■ More likely to go with the flow than stick to the timetable or the rules
■ Prefers to work in teams, flat hierarchies or self-employed than in hierarchical organisations or structured roles
■ Attracted to new or different ways of doing things
■ Tends to think more laterally and see novel connections
■ Can be disorganised
■ Can be late or unreliable at times
■ Can make impulsive, emotion-led decisions
■ Might find it hard to fit into other people's schedules or timetables
■ Can struggle to work in a straight line and finish tasks

Rigid–Dysregulated

- Depression, in particular, fixed negative beliefs
- Rumination, getting stuck on critical or distressing thoughts and ideas
- Not being able to allow feelings to come and go, shutting down internal experiences of feelings, getting panicky when feelings show up
- Getting stuck on anger, perceived injustices or slights
- Obsessing and being unable to shift thoughts and feelings unless they act in a particular way.
- Black and white thinking
- Rigid ideas of what is right and what is wrong, good or bad
- Derogatory ideas about others based on small flaws
- Racism, sexism or hate based on identity of others (scapegoating)
- Perfectionism, no tolerance for mistakes or not knowing
- Fearful or angry at lack of plans, other's lateness or imperfections
- Judgemental and critical thoughts about other's differences
- Habits or routines they don't want to do that end up feeling compulsive or like they aren't able to control themselves
- Addiction, rigid habitual use of drugs/alcohol
- Not being able to act spontaneously
- Excessive focus on tidiness, order, structure
- Demanding self-control and self-discipline from self
- Needing to control how others behave
- Attacking, criticising or demeaning others for how they act
- Violence, threats or abuse in an effort to get someone to stop doing things they don't like
- Tense muscles, rigid posture
- Breathing difficulties, trouble breathing deeply
- Exercising in ways that are excessive or harmful like training when injured or over-training
- Starving themself, withholding food or water
- Physical tension, back pain, neck pain, tension that can't be released
- Stomach aches, headaches or other physical signs of tension

Flexible–Dysregulated

■ Feeling like they've lost control of their mind or thinking
■ Intrusive thoughts, memories or ideas that are distressing and they can't control
■ Strong urges to act in ways that are self-destructive or harmful
■ Self-punishment via self-harm, literally hitting or attacking or causing self-physical harm, lashing out at self
■ Agitation or physical discomfort that makes it hard to sit still or relax
■ A feeling of wanting to cry or scream, or actually screaming/crying uncontrollably
■ Feeling like they can't think straight or follow things
■ Unable to read, or follow the plot in a movie or TV show
■ Thinking about more and more distressing things from the past
■ Having thoughts about bad things happening to people they care about
■ Thoughts about death, of themslves or others
■ Unable to stop worrying about the future
■ Knots in stomach, butterflies, feeling nauseous
■ Physical violence towards objects or things (hitting walls, throwing things)
■ Excessive alcohol or drug use leading to chaos
■ Bingeing on food
■ Impulsive decisions to do things that are harmful, or that we know are bad for us
■ Sexual impulsivity
■ Gambling excessively
■ Giggly, hysterical, or easily moved to incongruent laughing
■ Neglecting basic self-care like washing, dressing, eating meals
■ Feeling like they can't get on top of basic chores, excessively messy external or home environment
■ Unable to plan or structure tasks, activities or daily tasks
■ Easily distracted or diverted away from tasks
■ Easily overwhelmed by emotions into tearfulness, anger and yelling or other expressions of emotions.
■ Short temper, easily irritated or angry with self or others

Learning how to live "above the line"

In simple terms, living "above the line" means learning to regulate our emotional responses, and spending less and less time in a dysregulated state, or "below the line." Remember, that doesn't mean not experiencing emotions, or getting upset. It means feeling our emotions, without getting stuck, overwhelmed, or having our emotions distort our view of reality.

Towards balance

Ultimately, we can't avoid life. We also can't avoid having a childhood, psychological bumps and bruises, or even life-

---

Learnable skills from the Rigid-Regulated quadrant

- Mental focus and concentration
- Taking time to think before acting — slowing down
- Asking for advice from experts
- Finding comfort and safety in the certainty of the rules
- Structure, routine and predictable daily schedules
- Finding calm in predictability
- Good self-care in regular sleep, eating and exercise routines
- Seeking out and using reputable and reliable sources of information for decision making
- Researching before acting on big decisions
- Staying on task, doing one thing at a time
- Finishing a task or project before starting a new one
- Following instructions, reading manuals and recipes before starting
- Using rational thought-based approaches and mental skills to manage emotions i.e. CBT
- Making and using plans to help manage distress or challenging times
- Making commitments, goals and plans and sticking to them
- Setting, maintaining and communicating clear boundaries

changing traumas. Shit happens, as the cynical saying goes, but we can learn, adapt, and change. If you've experienced significant trauma or are just struggling with low mood and feeling stuck — all of us seek to find a way to manage our emotional world and return to balance.

In this map, then the centre point and balance are home. What is balance? In the simplest possible terms, it's when we are at peace with what is. It isn't necessarily an absence of upset, emotion, pain, distress, or difficult life events, but an acceptance of them. It's riding the rollercoaster of life, not fighting reality.

It's a deep openness to the experience of being alive. It's

Learnable skills from the Flexible-Regulated quadrant

■ Acceptance-based skills, working with what is, not what should be
■ Feeling emotions moment by moment, allowing feelings to come and go
■ Being open to new ideas, new ways of doing things, and other's points of view
■ Open to difference
■ Non-judgemental
■ Mindfulness-based approaches to just observing what is there
■ Changing plans when needed, not sticking to plans for the sake of it
■ Being able to use flow states to be in the moment and play
■ Dancing! (Like no one's watching)
■ Letting go of things, being present in the moment
■ Learning from doing, and being open to getting it wrong
■ Finding different ways to express things, through art, movement, music
■ Tolerating not knowing

the calm after the storm, the feeling of home, our children running to us and jumping into our arms, our lover's embrace.

It's home — literal and metaphorical.

It's home because balance is the place we keep returning to. As life happens, and emotions show up, regulated or dysregulated, and we respond, rigidly or flexibly, we keep working to return to balance, over and over again. Sometimes many times a day. It's not quite the same thing as being calm, which I think of as more the absence of emotional responses, but more a sense of not having to cope or respond because it just is. And we are safe and secure enough to let it be. (McCartney and Lennon again ...)

Of course, the more intense the event, and the more powerful the emotional response, the more it throws us away from balance — to the outer reaches of the map — maybe even off the page! And as a result, it requires more work, and probably more time, to return to a place of balance.

And while I've already explained that I don't see this map functioning as a replacement for a model of mental illness or a diagnostic framework, struggling to find balance is a pretty good description of acute mental distress.

To return to attachment theory, people who have experienced a secure attachment in childhood find stability and security more easily in adulthood. Having had a secure home inside themselves, they find it easier to return to balance when knocked by life's challenges. On the other hand, those whose experience of childhood was of disorganised attachment, the most severe of outcomes, are effectively psychologically homeless. Lacking this security and safety inside themselves they may struggle to ever find balance.

But even those psychologically homeless can find a place to settle. In therapy — or indeed in any relationship that offers them consistency, safety and a place to call home — even if only for one or two hours a week. And in therapy we may very well be building the house from the ground up, renovating a dilapidated old villa (sorry, a very "Auckland"example). Or our home may just need a quick lick of paint, but either way, balance can always be found, if we have someone to help us on the journey and a good enough map.

Index